# WALKING THE GR5: LAKE GENEVA TO MONT-BLANC

Titles in the Footpaths of Europe Series

The publishers thank the following people for permission to use their photographs in this book: J. Cantaloube, H. Viaux, J. M. Humeau, D. Fortunato.

# WALKING THE GR5: LAKE GENEVA TO MONT-BLANC

Translated by Simon Knight
in association with First Edition

Robertson McCarta

The publishers thank the following people for their help with this book: Isabelle Daguin, Philippe Lambert, Serge Sineux, Daphne Terry.

First published in 1990 by

**Robertson McCarta Limited**
122 King's Cross Road
London WC1X 9DS

in association with

**Fédération Française de la Randonnée Pédestre**
8 Avenue Marceau
75008 Paris

© Robertson McCarta Limited
© Fédération Française de Randonnée Pédestre
© Maps, Institut Geographique National (French Official Survey)
   and Robertson McCarta Limited.

**Managing Editor** Folly Marland
**Series designed** by Prue Bucknall
**Production** by Grahame Griffiths
**Typeset** by The Robertson Group, Llandudno
**Planning Map** by Rodney Paull

Printed and bound in Spain by Graficas Estella S.A.

British Library Cataloguing in Publication Data

Walking the GR5: Lake Geneva to Mont-Blanc. — (Footpaths of Europe).
   1. France. Mont-Blanc. Visitors' guides
   I. Series
   914.4'48

   ISBN 1-85365-109-5

Every care has been taken to ensure that all the information in this book is accurate. The publishers cannot accept any responsibility for any errors that may appear or their consequences.

# CONTENTS

# Key to IGN Maps

Motorway, dual carriageway _____

Major road, four lanes or more _____

Main road, two-lane or three-lane, wide _____

Main road, two-lane, narrow _____

Narrow road, regularly surfaced _____

Other narrow road: regularly surfaced; irregularly surfaced _____

Possibly private or controlled access

Field track, forest track, felling track, footpath _____

Track of disused road. Road under construction _____

Road through embankment, cutting. Tree-lined road or track _____

Bank. Hedge, line of trees _____

Railway: double track, single track. Electrified line. Station, waiting line. Halt, stop ____

Sidings or access lines. Narrow gauge line. Rack railway _____

Electricity transmission line. Cable railway. Ski lift _____

National boundary with markers _____

Boundary and administrative centre of department, district _____   **PF**   **SP**

Boundary and administrative centre of canton, commune _____   **CT**   **C**

For shooting times, go to town hall or gendarmerie

Boundary of military camp, firing range _____

Boundary of State forest, National Park, outer zone of National Park _____

Triangulation points _____

Church, chapel, shrine. Cross, tomb, religious statue. Cemetery _____

Watch tower, fortress. Windmill, wind-pump. Chimney _____   **Tr**   **Chem.**

Storage tank: oil, gas. Blast furnace. Pylon. Quarry _____

Cave. Monument, pillar. Castle. Ruins _____   **Mon.**   **P.V.**

Megalithic monument: dolmen, menhir. Viewpoint. Campsite _____

Market-hall, shed, glasshouse, casemate _____

Access to underground workings. Refuge. Ski-jump _____   **Mine**   **Cave**

Population/thousands _____   183,2   0,4   0,15   0,06

Bridge. Footbridge. Ford. Ferry _____

Lake, pool. Area liable to flooding. Marsh _____

Source, spring. Well, water-tank. Water-tower, reservoir _____   **Ch⁰ᵘ d'Eau**

Watercourse lined with trees. Waterfall. Dam. Dyke _____

Navigable canal, feeder or irrigator. Lock, machine-operated. Underground channel

Contour lines. 10 m. interval. Hollow. Small basin. Scree _____

| Woodland | Scrub | Orchard, plantation | Vines | Ricefield |

All maps are IGN Orange series. 1:50 000

© I.G.N. – Paris

Principal   Secondary

# A note from the publisher

The books in this French Walking Guide series are produced in association and with the help of the Fédération Française de la Randonnée Pédestre (French ramblers' association) — generally known as the FFRP.

The FFRP is a federal organisation and is made up of regional, local and many other associations and bodies that form its constituent parts. Individual membership is through these various local organisations. The FFRP therefore acts as an umbrella organisation overseeing the waymarking of footpaths, training and the publishing of the Topoguides, detailed guides to the Grande Randonnée footpaths.

There are at present about 170 Topoguides in print, compiled and written by local members of the FFRP, who are responsible for waymarking the walks — so they are well researched and accurate.

We have translated the main itinerary descriptions, amalgamating and adapting several Topoguides to create new regional guides. We have retained the basic Topoguide structure, indicating length and times of walks, and the Institut Géographique National (official French survey) maps overlaid with the routes.

The information contained in this guide is the latest available at the time of going to print. However, as publishers we are aware that this kind of information is continually changing and we are anxious to enhance and improve the guides as much as possible. We encourage you to send us suggestions, criticisms and those little bits of information you may wish to share with your fellow walkers. Our address is: Robertson McCarta, 122 King's Cross Road, London WC1X 9DS.

We shall be happy to offer a free copy of any one of these books to any reader whose suggestions are subsequently incorporated into a new edition.

It is possible to create a variety of routes by referring to the walks in the contents page and to the planning map (inside the front cover). Transport is listed in the alphabetical index at the back of the book and there is an accommodation guide.

# KEY

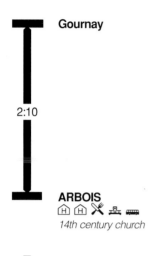

**Gournay**

This example shows that you can expect the walk from Gournay to Arbois to take 2 hours, 10 minutes.

2:10

**ARBOIS**
14th century church

Arbois has a variety of facilities, including hotels and buses. Hotel addresses and bus/train connections may be listed in the index at the back of the book.

A grey arrow indicates an alternative route that leaves and returns to the main route.

**Detour**

indicates a short detour off the route to a town with facilities or to an interesting sight.

---

**Symbols:**

| | |
|---|---|
| ⌂ hotel; | 🏬 shops; |
| △ youth hostel, hut or refuge; | 🚃 railway station; |
| ▲ camping; | 🚌 buses; |
| ✗ restaurant; | ⛴ ferry; |
| ♐ cafe; | 🛈 tourist information; |

# THE FOOTPATHS OF FRANCE

by Robin Neillands

**W**hy should you go walking in France? Well, walking is fun and as for France, Danton summed up the attractions of that country with one telling phrase: 'Every man has two countries,' he said, 'his own . . . and France.' That is certainly true in my case and I therefore consider it both a pleasure and an honour to write this general introduction to these footpath guides to France. A pleasure because walking in or through France is my favourite pastime, an honour because these excellent English language guides follow in the course set by those Topo-guides published in French by the Fédération Française pour la Randonnée Pédestre, which set a benchmark for quality that all footpath guides might follow. Besides, I believe that good things should be shared and walking in France is one of the most pleasant activities I know.

I have been walking in France for over thirty years. I began by rambling — or rather ambling — through the foothills of the Pyrenees, crossing over into Spain past the old Hospice de France, coming back over the Somport Pass in a howling blizzard, which may account for the fact that I totally missed two sets of frontier guards on both occasions. Since then I have walked in many parts of France and even from one end of it to the other, from the Channel to the Camargue, and I hope to go on walking there for many years to come.

The attractions of France are legion, but there is no finer way to see and enjoy them than on foot. France has two coasts, at least three mountain ranges — the Alps, Pyrenees and the Massif Central — an agreeable climate, a great sense of space, good food, fine wines and, believe it or not, a friendly and hospitable people. If you don't believe me, go there on foot and see for yourself. Walking in France will appeal to every kind of walker, from the day rambler to the backpacker, because above all, and in the nicest possible way, the walking in France is well organised, but those Francophiles who already know France well will find it even more pleasurable if they explore their favourite country on foot.

## The GR system

The Grande Randonnée (GR) footpath network now consists of more than 40,000 kilometres (25,000 miles) of long-distance footpath, stretching into every part of France, forming a great central sweep around Paris, probing deeply into the Alps, the Pyrenees, and the volcanic cones of the Massif Central. This network, the finest system of footpaths in Europe, is the creation of that marvellously named organisation, *la Fédération Française de Randonnée Pédestre, Comité National des Sentiers de Grande Randonnée,* which I shall abbreviate to FFRP-CNSGR. Founded in 1948, and declaring that, *'un jour de marche, huit jours de santé'* the FFRP-CNSGR has flourished for four decades and put up the now familiar red-and -white waymarks in every corner of the country. Some of these footpaths are classic walks, like the famous GR65, *Le Chemin de St. Jacques,* the ancient Pilgrim Road to Compostela, the TMB, the *Tour du Mont Blanc,* which circles the mountain through France,

Switzerland and Italy, or the 600-mile long GR3, the *Sentier de la Loire,* which runs from the Ardèche to the Atlantic, to give three examples from the hundred or so GR trails available. In addition there is an abundance of GR du Pays or regional footpaths, like the *Sentier de la Haute Auvergne,* and the *Sentier Tour des Monts d'Aubrac.* A 'Tour' incidentally, is usually a circular walk. Many of these regional or provincial GR trails are charted and waymarked in red-and-yellow by local outdoor organisations such as ABRI (Association Bretonne des Relais et Itineraires) for Brittany, or CHAMINA for the Massif Central. The walker in France will soon become familiar with all these footpath networks, national, regional or local, and find them the perfect way into the heart and heartland of France. As a little bonus, the GR networks are expanding all the time, with the detours — or *varientes* — off the main route eventually linking with other GR paths or *varientes* and becoming GR trails in their own right.

Walkers will find the GR trails generally well marked and easy to follow, and they have two advantages over the footpaths commonly encountered in the UK. First, since they are laid out by local people, they are based on intricate local knowledge of the local sights. If there is a fine view, a mighty castle or a pretty village on your footpath route, your footpath through France will surely lead you to it. Secondly, all French footpaths are usually well provided with a wide range of comfortable country accommodation, and you will discover that the local people, even the farmers, are well used to walkers and greet them with a smile, a *'Bonjour'* and a *'bonne route'.*

## Terrain and Climate

As a glance at these guides or any Topo-guide will indicate, France has a great variety of terrain. France is twice the size of the UK and many natural features are also on a larger scale. There are three main ranges of mountains, the Alps contain the highest mountain in Europe, the Pyrenees go up to 10,000 ft, the Massif Central peaks to over 6000 ft, and there are many similar ranges with hills which overtop our highest British peak, Ben Nevis. On the other hand, the Auvergne and the Jura have marvellous open ridge walking, the Cévennes are steep and rugged, the Ardeche and parts of Provence are hot and wild, the Île de France, Normandy, Brittany and much of Western France is green and pleasant, not given to extremes. There is walking in France for every kind of walker, but given such a choice the wise walker will consider the complications of terrain and weather before setting out, and go suitably equipped.

France enjoys three types of climate: continental, oceanic, and mediterranean. South of the Loire it will certainly be hot to very hot from mid-April to late September. Snow can fall on the mountains above 4000 ft from mid-October and last until May, or even lie year-round on the tops and in couloirs; in the high hills an ice-axe is never a frill. I have used one by the Brêche de Roland in the Pyrenees in mid-June.

Wise walkers should study weather maps and forecasts carefully in the week before they leave for France, but can generally expect good weather from May to October, and a wide variety of weather — the severity depending on the terrain — from mid-October to late Spring.

## Accommodation

The walker in France can choose from a wide variety of accommodation with the asurance that the walker will always be welcome. This can range from country hotels to wild mountain pitches, but to stay in comfort, many walkers will travel light and overnight in the comfortable hotels of the *Logis de France* network.

*Logis de France:* The *Logis de France* is a nationwide network of small, family-run country hotels, offering comfortable accommodation and excellent food. *Logis* hotels are graded and can vary from a simple, one-star establishment, with showers and linoleum, to a four- or five-star *logis* with gastronomic menus and deep pile-carpets. All offer excellent value for money, and since there are over 5,000 scattered across the French countryside, they provide a good focus for a walking day. An annual guide to the *Logis* is available from the French Government Tourist Office, 178 Piccadilly, London W1V 0AL, Tel (01) 491 7622.

*Gîtes d'étape:* A *gîte d'étape* is best imagined as an unmanned youth hostel for outdoor folk of all ages. They lie along the footpath networks and are usually signposted or listed in the guides. They can be very comfortable, with bunk beds, showers, a well equipped kitchen, and in some cases they have a warden, a *guardien,* who may offer meals. *Gîtes d'étape* are designed exclusively for walkers, climbers, cyclists, cross country skiers or horse-riders. A typical price (1990) would be Fr.25 for one night. *Gîtes d'étape* should not be confused with a *Gîte de France.* A *gîte* — usually signposted as *'Gîte de France'* — is a country cottage available for a holiday let, though here too, the owner may be more than willing to rent it out as overnight accommodation.

*Youth hostels:* Curiously enough, there are very few Youth Hostels in France outside the main towns. A full list of the 200 or so available can be obtained from the Youth Hostel Association (YHA), Trevelyan House, St. Albans, Herts AL1 2DY.

*Pensions or cafes:* In the absence of an hotel, a *gîte d'étape* or a youth hostel, all is not lost. France has plenty of accommodation and an enquiry at the village cafe or bar will usually produce a room. The cafe/hotel may have rooms or suggest a nearby pension or a *chambre d'hôte.* Prices start at around Fr.50 for a room, rising to say, Fr.120. (1990 estimate).

*Chambres d'hôte:* A *chambre d'hôte* is a guest room, or, in English terms, a bed-and-breakfast, usually in a private house. Prices range from about Fr.60 a night. *Chambres d'hôte* signs are now proliferating in the small villages of France and especially if you can speak a little French are an excellent way to meet the local people. Prices (1990) are from, say, Fr.70 for a room, not per person.

*Abris: Abris,* shelters or mountain huts can be found in the mountain regions, where they are often run by the *Club Alpin Francais,* an association for climbers. They range from the comfortable to the primitive, are often crowded and are sometimes reserved for members. Details from the Club Alpin Francais, 7 Rue la Boétie, Paris 75008, France.

*Camping:* French camp sites are graded from one to five star, but are generally very good at every level, although the facilities naturally vary from one cold tap to shops, bars and heated pools. Walkers should not be deterred by the *'Complet'* (Full) sign on the gate or office window: a walker's small tent will usually fit in somewhere. *Camping à la ferme,* or farm camping, is increasingly popular, more primitive — or less regimented — than the official sites, but widely available and perfectly adequate. Wild camping is officially not permitted in National Parks, but unofficially if you are over 1,500m away from a road, one hour's walk from a *gîte* or campsite, and where possible ask permission, you should have no trouble. French country people will always assist the walker to find a pitch.

## The law for walkers
The country people of France seem a good deal less concerned about their 'rights' than the average English farmer or landowner. I have never been ordered off land in France or greeted with anything other than friendliness . . . maybe I've been lucky. As a rule, walkers in France are free to roam over all open paths and tracks. No decent walker will leave gates open, trample crops or break down walls, and taking fruit from gardens or orchards is simply stealing. In some parts of France there are local laws about taking chestnuts, mushrooms (and snails), because these are cash crops. Signs like *Réserve de Chasse*, or *Chasse Privé* indicate that the shooting is reserved for the landowner. As a general rule, behave sensibly and you will be tolerated everywhere, even on private land.

## The country code
Walkers in France should obey the *Code du Randonneur.*

- Love and respect nature.
- Avoid unnecessary noise.
- Destroy nothing.
- Do not leave litter.
- Do not pick flowers or plants.
- Do not disturb wildlife.
- Re-close all gates.
- Protect and preserve the habitat.
- No smoking or fires in the forests. (This rule is essential and is actively enforced by foresters and police).
- Respect and understand the country way of life and the country people.
- Think of others as you think of yourself.

## Transport
Transportation to and within France is generally excellent. There are no less than nine Channel ports: Dunkirk, Calais, Boulogne, Dieppe, Le Havre, Caen/Ouistreham, Cherbourg, Saint-Malo and Roscoff, and a surprising number of airports served by direct flights from the UK. Although some of the services are seasonal, it is often possible to fly direct to Toulouse, Poitiers, Nantes, Perpignan, Montpellier, indeed to many provincial cities, as well as Paris and such obvious destinations as Lyon and Nice. Within France the national railway, the SNCF, still retains a nationwide network. Information, tickets and a map can be obtained from the SNCF. France also has a good country bus service and the *gare routière* is often placed just beside the railway station. Be aware though, that many French bus services only operate within the *département,* and they do not generally operate from one provincial city to the next. I cannot encourage people to hitch-hike, which is both illegal and risky, but walkers might consider a taxi for their luggage. Almost every French village has a taxi driver who will happily transport your rucksacks to the next night-stop, fifteen to twenty miles away, for Fr.50 a head or even less.

## Money

Walking in France is cheap, but banks are not common in the smaller villages, so carry a certain amount of French money and the rest in traveller's cheques or Eurocheques, which are accepted everywhere.

## Clothing and equipment

The amount of clothing and equipment you will need depends on the terrain, the length of the walk, the time of your visit, the accommodation used. Outside the mountain areas it is not necessary to take the full range of camping or backpacking gear. I once walked across France from the Channel to the Camargue along the Grande Randonneé footpaths in March, April and early May and never needed to use any of the camping gear I carried in my rucksack because I found hotels everywhere, even in quite small villages.

Essential items are:
**In summer:** light boots, a hat, shorts, suncream, lip salve, mosquito repellent, sunglasses, a sweater, a windproof cagoule, a small first-aid kit, a walking stick.
**In winter:** a change of clothing, stormproof outer garments, gaiters, hat, lip salve, a companion.
**In the mountains at any time:** large-scale maps (1:25,000), a compass, an ice-axe. In winter, add a companion and ten-point crampons.
**At any time:** a phrase book, suitable maps, a dictionary, a sense of humour.

The best guide to what to take lies in the likely weather and the terrain. France tends to be informal, so there is no need to carry a jacket or something smart for the evenings. I swear by Rohan clothing, which is light, smart and functional. The three things I would never go without are light, well-broken-in boots and several pairs of loop-stitched socks, and my walking stick.

## Health hazards:

Health hazards are few. France can be hot in summer, so take a full water-bottle and refill at every opportunity. A small first-aid kit is sensible, with plasters and 'mole-skin' for blisters, but since prevention is better than the cure, loop-stitched socks and flexible boots are better. Any French chemist — a *pharmacie* — is obliged to render first-aid treatment for a small fee. These pharmacies can be found in most villages and large towns and are marked by a green cross.

Dogs are both a nuisance and a hazard. All walkers in France should carry a walking stick to fend off aggressive curs. Rabies — *la rage* — is endemic and any-one bitten must seek immediate medical advice. France also possesses two types of viper, which are common in the hill areas of the south. In fairness, although I found my walking stick indispensable, I must add that in thirty years I have never even seen a snake or a rabid dog. In case of real difficulty, dial 17 for the police and the ambulance.

## Food and wine

One of the great advantages with walking in France is that you can end the day with a good meal and not gain an ounce. French country cooking is generally excellent and good value for money, with the price of a four-course menu starting at about Fr.45. The ingredients for the mid-day picnic can be purchased from the village shops and these also sell wine. Camping-Gaz cylinders and cartridges are widely available, as is 2-star petrol for stoves. Avoid naked fires.

## Preparation

The secret of a good walk lies in making adequate preparations before you set out. It pays to be fit enough to do the daily distance at the start. Much of the necessary information is contained in this guide, but if you need more, look in guidebooks or outdoor magazines, or ask friends.

## The French

I cannot close this introduction without saying a few words about the French, not least because the walker in France is going to meet rather more French people than, say, a motorist will, and may even meet French people who have never met a foreigner before. It does help if the visitor speaks a little French, even if only to say *'bonjour'* and *'Merci'* and *'S'il vous plait'*. The French tend to be formal so it pays to be polite, to say 'hello', to shake hands. I am well aware that relations between France and England have not always been cordial over the last six hundred years or so, but I have never met with hostility of any kind in thirty years of walking through France. Indeed, I have always found that if the visitor is prepared to meet the French halfway, they will come more than halfway to greet him or her in return, and are both friendly and hospitable to the passing stranger.

As a final tip, try smiling. Even in France, or especially in France, a smile and a *'pouvez vous m'aider?'* (Can you help me?) will work wonders. That's my last bit of advice, and all I need do now is wish you *'Bonne Route'* and good walking in France.

# THE GR5

by Henri Viot,

*President of the French Ramblers Association,1977-1989*

The systematic development of long-distance walking in France dates from the immediate post-war period, when two important societies - the Touring Club de France and the Club Alpin Français - began using substantial numbers of volunteers to establish a network of footpaths covering the whole country. These routes became known as 'Sentiers de Grande Randonnée' - 'long-distance footpaths' - soon abbreviated to the simple title of 'GR', each linear or circular route having its own identifying number. The principal aim of the GR paths was to make the best possible use of paths and tracks barred to motorised vehicles, and to reveal rural France in all its richness and variety - the natural wealth of upland and lowland landscapes, the human interest of traditional rural life, and the inherited magnificence of buildings and monuments - combined with enjoyable physical activity. France's mountains have naturally provided an important element of the network. Standardised waymarking was designed to encourage familiarity and confidence in walking: the markings consist of two bars, one red and one white, painted on to any permanent feature along the route.

One of the first footpaths to be planned and established was the GR5, crossing the whole of eastern France from the Luxembourg frontier to the Mediterranean coast on the Côte d'Azur, via the principal mountain massifs - the Vosges, Jura, and the Alps. The route was later extended through Belgium to Ostend.

Completion of the route took a long time, but the most important section, across the Alps - already well-known to climbers, and using traditional tracks familiar to shepherds, itinerant traders, and armies on the march - was soon mapped out and established. The Savoy section of the GR5 was opened to walkers in 1955, extending in due course to Nice and Menton on the Côte d'Azur.

Complementary circular routes were established at the same time in the main mountain massifs, enabling walkers to explore the remote inner mountain areas in greater detail. These too are important GR routes; from north to south, they are: the Tour du Mont-Blanc, across the Vanoise (GR55), the Ecrins - Oisans massif (GR54), the Queyras massif (GR58), the Ubaye massif (GR56), and the Mercantour (GR52).

All these GR routes follow moderate mountain altitudes, between approximately 1,000 and 1,500 metres; any reasonably fit walker can thus explore these great mountain areas without the need for specialised mountaineer equipment. The footpaths lead from col to col and valley to valley, through villages and hamlets where the traditional rural pattern of mountain life still persists almost unchanged: in the mountains it is nature - topography and climate - which commands, and mankind who obeys. Conditions are hard at these high altitudes, demanding endurance and experience and not suited to everyone in primitive huts alongside the flocks in their alpine pastures. For the urban holiday-maker who walks these paths, the encounter with such a way of life can be enlightening and thought-provoking. Nature too has much to reveal to the visitor; summer months bring the delights of flowering alpine meadows, inspiration of the 'mille-fleurs' tapestries. Animal and bird life in the mountains is no less fascinating, for those who are prepared to get up early and go equipped with a good pair of binoculars and plenty of patience: marmots, chamois and ibex can all be seen at various stages along the route, there may be rare birds such as eagles and grouse, the choughs, finches, and many forms of passerines are commonplace. In Autumn walkers can enjoy wild raspberries, bilberries, and mushrooms.

Walking the GR5 and its branches demands a sound pair of lungs and good leg muscles; and will specially interest those with a lively curiosity concerning all aspects of nature - though few could walk such a route without being fascinated by its flora and geological structure, and its resident animal life.

Romantic writers of the mid-nineteenth century who discovered the Chamonix Valley, the gateway to the upper Alps, spoke of 'these sublime and terrible mountains'. Human attitudes to the mountains have changed since then, and no-one now would dare to call them terrible; but for the walker who follows the GR5 on a fine summer's day, past majestic rock faces, snow-fields and towering glaciers, the mountains remain truly sublime.

### The GR5, North
The northern Alpine section of the GR5 goes through the départements of Haute-Savoie and Savoie, making up the historic province of Savoy which in 1860 voted to become part of France. This is the region of the true Alps, with Mont Blanc their highest peak. The GR5 crosses the area at a relatively modest altitude; starting from Lake Geneva (Lac Léman), the path climbs gently up through the Chablais meadows to the Col d'Anterne, its first high pass. The descent through the Chamonix valley reveals the magnificent ensemble of the Mont Blanc massif; the path curves round to the west of Mont Blanc, southwards to the Vanoise massif and its National Park. Along the way two mountains - from the Tarentaise valley to the Maurienne valley. From the latter the path climbs up to the Vallée Etroite which marks the climatic frontier of the southern Alps.

On its way the GR5 shares its route for some way with the internationally famous Tour du Mont-Blanc GR, which crosses various cols at or above an altitude of 2,500 metres and runs into Italy and Switzerland, with extraordinary views of the great faces and glaciers of the roof of Europe. The route through the Col de Balme to Brévent via the Balcon de la Flégère is one of the most impressive in the whole Alpine massif.

### The GR5, South
On leaving Savoy the GR5 goes over the Col de la Vallée Etroite, the climatic threshold of the southern Alps. Here it embarks on a series of mountainous massifs slightly lower than the northern Alps and offering less austere landscapes with the welcoming Névache valley as a typical introductory example. Next the route crosses the Regional Nature Park of the Queyras massif; it is rewarding to turn off at Saint-Véran or Ceillac to walk the GR58 which explores all areas of the National Park.

After crossing the Ubaye massif and the Haute-Tinée, the GR5 enters the National Park of the Mercantour massif in Haute Provence; here it divides in two, one branch leading to Nice and the other to Menton with distant views over the Mediterranean. Here too there is good reason to make a detour, to enjoy the newly established GR of the Mercantour Panorama.

First, however, the GR5 passes the Ecrins National Park, to the left and on a level with Briançon. The Ecrins Park has two important, circular GR routes: the high mountain GR54 path, demanding and occasionally bleak, dominated by impressive rock faces including La Meije; and the GR50, the Tour du Haut-Dauphiné, less strenuous, but offering magnificent glimpses of the high Ecrins peaks.

# The Haute-Savoie section of the GR5

L ake Geneva to Mont-Blanc .... a title to stir the imagination tempting you to venture forth on the Haute-Savoie stretch of the GR5. And you will not be disappointed: the path leads you into regions of distinctly individual character, with frequent changes of mood, as it makes its way through the different stages of mountain landscape.

As you go, you will discover a variety of natural features:
● deep gorges and valleys, one side quite different from the other;
● warm, south-facing slopes and cliffs which shelter a number of localized bird species and flowers on the northern limits of their range;
● specialized types of environment, such as dry meadows, dunes on the shores of Lake Geneva, moraines of boulder clay, set in the typical wooded farmland of the Savoy foothills;
● peat bogs and other marshy areas, which are relics of the ice ages, and now a refuge for unique plants and animals, acting as sponges when the spring thaw comes;
● massive geological structures, limestone plateaux with complex underground water systems, deeply divided mountain massifs containing within themselves a variety of contrasting environments and types of animal and plant life.

We should also mention glacial systems deriving from rock formations not found elsewhere in France or even in Europe as a whole, for example the large and smaller glaciers retained by inertia in the limestone mountains of the Haut Giffre. Then there is Lake Geneva, the biggest lake in western Europe, and Mont-Blanc, highest peak of the continent.

As you follow the GR5 and local paths there are discoveries to be made at every step.

Leaving Lake Geneva, the GR enters the Pre-Alps of the Chablais region, with two possible routes from the lakeside to the Col de Bise:
1. the main route starts from Saint Gingolph on the Franco-Swiss frontier and, sticking close to the border in the Nouvel valley, climbs sharply towards Neuteu and Bise.
2. the so-called Thonon Alternative Route - positioned first in this guide as being easier of access by road and rail from most parts of France - is more pastoral in character. It climbs gradually up through the Thonon forest, crosses the Dranse and reaches Bise via Pelluaz and the magnificent massif and Portes de la Dent d'Oche, which open the way to the beauty of lake Darbon.

From here, you continue to the delightful Abondance valley, skirt the eastern slopes of the limestone pyramid of Mont de Grange, which is a game reserve, and, at the Col de Chésery, cross into the Swiss canton of Valais. You cross back into France by the Col de Coux, and on into the Faucigny region via the Col de Golèse. The resort of Samoëns is a perfect spot to break your journey before undertaking the steep climb up to the Col d'Anterne, passing frequent waterfalls on your way. To the West, the Rochers des Fiz look like an impregnable fortress, and at the pass itself you have your first full sight of the Mont-Blanc chain. Then a long climb over the scree brings you to the Col du Brévent in the region of rounded, snow-capped summits and granite peaks celebrated in the writings of Frison-Roche.

Here the GR5 joins forces with the Mont-Blanc Circular Route, the GRTMB, and descends steeply towards Les Houches and the Chamonix valley. Picking its way among the huge construction sites of the Route Blanche or White motorway, the path then rises gently to the Col de Voza or the Col de Tricot, and on into the Val Montjoie.

After les Contamines, as you climb upwards to the Col de la Croix-du-Bonhomme, you are walking on the Rochassets trail, a route trodden two thousand years ago by the Roman legions.

From this vantage point, you can, if you wish, continue your journey along the GR5 into Savoy and on to the distant Mediterranean, or you can take the TMB down into the Val d'Aosta and so into Italy.

Whichever way you take, I am sure we shall meet again some day on one of the spellbinding footpaths of Haute-Savoie. Until then, farewell and watch your step.

**Georges HYVERNAT**
*Chairman of CODERANDO 74*

# Please note

In both France and Switzerland, many alpine pastures are enclosed, with gates across tracks and footpaths. Please take care to close all gates after you, and leave domestic animals to graze undisturbed.

Always remember that whereas, for you, the summer is a time of rest and relaxation, for alpine farmers and graziers it means hard work and the struggle for survival. They have to produce high-quality produce, look after the land, build defences against avalanches - responsibilities they have been undertaking for generations. Mountain agriculture is a hard way of life, but too important to be allowed to die out.

Often, at the times of year when they are down in the valleys, the mountain folk leave a chalet or room open for others to shelter in. Take advantage of this kindness if you are overtaken by bad weather, but do not light a fire: having his chalet burnt down is one of the nightmares of the alpine grazier.

Do not pick flowers; leave them for others to enjoy. In Haute-Savoie and in the Valais region, many species are protected and by picking them you make yourself punishable by law. In nature reserves, this applies to all species.

## Breaking your journey

How you break up your journey will depend upon your physical fitness and your choice of accommodation. Have a look at the estimated walking times and facilities available en route. The times shown for lowland and valley sections are for a person walking at a steady rate of 4 kilometres an hour. However, individual walkers, especially campers, should take into account the amount of equipment they are carrying and their physical condition. Times for steep mountain paths have been calculated differently: 300 metres per hour on uphill sections and 400 to 500 metres coming down, for a walker with a small or medium-sized load.

## Difficulties

The GR5 footpath and the Portes du Soleil and Dents du Midi Circular Routes all run through middle-mountain terrain, at altitudes ranging from 386 metres at Saint Gingolph to 2,494 metres at the Col de Susanfe and 2,526 metres at the Brévent. They are therefore suitable for ramblers who are fit and experienced in mountain walking with a backpack.

The GR and its alternative routes always follow an existing, marked way: footpath, trail, mule track or section of road. Nevertheless, when they cross grassy areas, in woods or especially in alpine meadowland, the course of the path is often hard to make out. In this case, go strictly by the descriptions in the guidebook. The routes described are quite safe, except in bad weather: fog, snow - which may fall even in summer - and storms, or at times other than the summer months. Negotiating a mountain pass or stream, though easy in summer, can become tricky or even dangerous when there is snow or ice on the ground. In wet weather or after a fall or rain, rocks and grass can be very slippery; in autumn, there is the risk of slipping on wet leaves. Warning is given in the guide at points where any of these dangers are especially likely to occur. Early in the season, if you have to negotiate a snowfall or unmelted ice, a light ice-axe is worth carrying. Finally, take extra care when walking along a ridge.

## Time of year

On these routes, in years when snowfalls have been moderate, the passes can be negotiated towards the end of May, though some hostels are not open until later in the season. The best time is from mid-June until the end of August, when the days are long, the alpine meadows in flower, and hostels open. September and October too can be very pleasant; you can see great distances in the clear air, but the days are shorter and hostels sometimes closed.

## Detours and excursions

The guidebook mentions some peaks which lie off the GR route. Some unmarked sections of path are also easy to find. Always be cautious and on your guard when venturing off the beaten track, and be sure you know how to read a map and use your compass and altimeter.

# WALK 1

**THONON-LES-BAINS**

🏠 ⛺ 🏕 🍴 🍷 🚋 🚌

🚌 🛈

*431m*

*(see map ref A)*

*Thonon, a resort on the southern shore of Lake Geneva, takes pride in being the most athletic town in France; in the Stone and Bronze ages, a village was built on piles on the present harbour site; the Romans discovered the health-giving properties of a local spring and a spa was born; before setting out walkers may like to relax and enjoy the facilities of the spa, or visit Rives to see the fishing port and its famous sentry boxes in the museum; other attractions include the basilica dedicated to Saint Francis de Sales; the church of Saint Hippolyte, which has a romanesque crypt with 3 vaults; viewpoints; the Châteaux of Sonnaz, now the museum of the Chablais region, and Bellegarde with its roguish carved wooden friezes; the Versoie Fountain; further east, the 14th century Château de Ripaille.*

0:40

**Lane to La Vionnaz**

*(see map ref B)*

*Vionnaz is pronounced Vionne.*

The walk starts on the GR5 Alternative Route from Thonon-les-Bains to the junction with the GR5 from Saint-Gingolph

The GR5 starts to the right of the railway station, in Rue J. Blanchard. There is a footbridge across the tracks, to the Place de Crête with its obelisk in honour of Napoleon's troops, who passed through the town during his Italian campaign. Cross the square southwards and take the lane to Trossy, which will bring you to Thonon Forest - at 490 metres - also known as the bois de ville.

**Warning** Here and further on, do not confuse the GR waymarks with forestry signs - red border on a white background - delimiting blocks of woodland.

Follow the path until you come to the lane to La Vionnaz.

Here, the local GR Littoral Léman rive Français joins the GR5 which continues on the level, then turns westward to the left, taking a track to the edge of the forest. Climb to the right

**1:10**

*Le Comte Rouge was the 14th century Count Amadeus VII of Savoy who earned this nickname by his daring military exploits: he would return from battle, his armour drenched with English blood!*

## ARMOY

*645m
(see map ref C)
Local inhabitants are known as Armoisiens; Romans set up an arms depot on the site of present presbytery; church of ancient origin, choir and presbytery dating from 1085; transept demolished during the French Revolution; rebuilt, then burned down in 1913 when a fire ravaged the whole village, sparing only choir of the church and presbytery.*

**1:45**

through a low growth of oak, hornbeam and chestnut, until you come to the road to l'Ermitage at 527 metres. Cross the road and climb up to an enclosed area shaded by cedars which used to be a nursery garden. The GR follows a road skirting the enclosure to the south and, after 100 metres, turns left on to the nursery track. Passing a forest shelter, it continues uphill to the right through an oak and beech wood. The path climbs through 2 hairpin bends to the edge of a terrace of glacial origin with a panoramic view. The GR turns left, then immediately right on to a track called the chemin des lapins with a nearby line of larches. After crossing the track to La Lonnaz, the path plunges down into a wooded combe, then climbs up again eastwards and to the left to the crossroads of Le Comte Rouge.

Continue until you come to a tarmac track, the old Thonon-Armoy road, and follow it to the right until you come to the D26 road. Turn left along the road, then off to the right and southwards on to a wide path. At the next crossing, the GR5 continues south, first through woods, then skirting farmland, eventually reaching the foot of the Montagne d'Hermone and the village of Armoy.

The GR passes below the church and carries straight on, eastwards, along a forest track; 100 metres further on, it starts to climb south-eastwards to the right, up to the edge of the ancient bois de Cure - communal woodland formerly at the village priest's disposal for firewood. The path continues between farmland and forest, coming to a place with views over the Dranse valley and, beyond, towards Tréchauffeux, 1,627 metres, and La Dent d'Oche, 2,222 metres. The next stretch is a broad dirt track, which bears left and to the south. At the first combe, the GR rejoins the woodland edge and follows it to connect up with another wide track. It next turns right on to a cart track which climbs a ridge, shaded by pine trees, and brings you out on to the D26. Turn right along the road, then turn left and take the road south east to the Jossières crossroads, where there is an oratory. Carry on along the road, then take a cart track, first

**Junction**
*856m*

0:50

**REYVROZ**
⌂ Å ⚒
*842m*
*(see map ref D)*
*A native of Reyvroz is a Reyvèrand.*

0:40

**BIOGE**
Å
*620m*
*This hamlet belongs partly to Reyvroz, partly to La Vernaz and partly to Féternes, at the confluence of the Dranse d'Abondance, Dranse de Morzine and Dranse de Bellevaux, or Brevon, rivers, before they plunge into deep gorges and flow out into Lake Geneva.*

1:00

to the east, then south east. The way leads gradually uphill between hedges, then through woodland, overlooking the D26. You pass close by the Chapelle des Pas and reach the crossroads at Bois de la Croix. Carry straight on, until you come to the junction.

The GR Balcon du Léman joins the GR5 Alternative Route on the right, where there is an oratory. The 2 GRs follow the same route as far as Les Lacs de la Case. Continue southwards, to the church of Reyvroz.

The path passes in front of the church, skirts the cemetery and goes down through the village. Cross the D26 crossroads and follow the road towards Vers-le-Pré. Taking a track downhill, then a pathway, with care you cut across high sandy slopes above the Brevon stream. Join the former Thonon-Morzine road, a pleasant, but sometimes a wet route, which will bring you to Bioge.

Turn right and cross the Brevon; when you reach the D902, turn right, follow the road for 300 metres, then turn left and cross the Dranse by a 17th-century stone bridge. Follow the D22 to the right (eastwards) for 100 metres, then turn right, just after the hydro-electric power station.

Cross the Dranse d'Abondance by the recently-repaired footbridge. A narrow, winding path brings you to a water supply point, then you cut across the meadows to arrive at La Forclaz, an outlying hamlet of Pombourg. Pass through, then take the track to the next hamlet, Chevenoz, looking down on the Dranse as you go.

Take the road to the left (eastwards), and 700 metres further on, turn off left onto the track to Plainesserve. A road on your right then brings you back to the D122, and so to Le Fion.

**Le Fion**
*809m*

0:15

**D22 road**

0:50

**CHEVENOZ**
Ⓗ ⌂ ⚓
*810m*
*(see map ref E)*

1:30

*From this vantage point,
there is a panoramic view of
Le Jura, Lake Geneva and,
in the foreground to the
north, the vast Gavot
plateau dominating the
Evian. To the north east is
the massive bulk of the
Mémises.*

**Le Petit Chesnay**
*1,336m*
**Detour** *15 mins*
**Tête des Trables or
Trêches**
*1,423m*
*If you walk along the grassy
shoulder to the south west
above the chalets, you can
easily reach the summit.
There is a cross on the
summit and a magnificent
view all around.*

In the village, the GR turns left onto the D222, northwards, cuts across the bends in the road, descends into the valley and crosses the Dranse d'Abondance at the Pont du Moulin. From the bridge, the path climbs up again to the D22 road.

Follow the road uphill. At the first bend, turn off, northwards across meadows, until you come to the D32 at Chevenoz.

Follow the D22 road to the left for a short distance, then take another road to your right, northwards. Turn off, 50 metres further on to a footpath which cuts across the hairpin bends in the road, climbs up to Chez Pollien and joins another path leading behind a fountain with a massive trough, dated 1861. From here, you climb up through woodland and through 2 gates towards Les Moliets. After 600 metres take a track on your right, with a reservoir on your left, and 500 metres further on, after a hairpin bend to the left, climb up out of the forest. Make sure the gate is properly closed. You have now emerged on to the alpine meadowland and farms of Sur les Trables, 1,115 metres high.

The GR continues upwards and to the east across the slope, first through meadowland, then in the woods. A steeper stretch brings you to the high-alpine chalets of Le Petit Chesnay.

The GR5 continues, eastwards, to the farm at Le Grand Chesnay at 1,414 metres.

**0:20**

The chalet, with a shingle roof, is used during the summer grazing period. Note the view to the south of the slender peak of Mont Ouzon, 1,881 metres high. From here, there are views to the east of Mont Baron in the foreground and, in the distance, the striking shape of La Dent d'Oche and the Roc du Château d'Oche.

The path skirts the northern side of a grassy mound and passes a cross.

**Warning** It is easy to lose the way on this stretch, since there is nothing to fix waymarks to.

The GR proceeds through pastureland, climbing south south-eastwards on a poorly defined path. It negotiates a rock and leads through a wood before emerging into a grassy pass.

**Grassy pass**
**Detour** 15 mins
**Le Mont-Baron**
1,556m
North east, to the left, there is a pathway up the slope to the summit. To rejoin the GR, you can either retrace your steps or come back down by the grassy ridge to the south east.

**0:35**

Do not go downhill to the right, but take a pathway eastwards across the slope which leads down to the foot of the cliffs on the south face of Mont Baron and to the Col des Boeufs at 1,436 metres. The path then climbs to the south south east close to the Crêtes des Grandes Heures, the ridges forming the dividing line between the communes of Bernex and Vacheresse. When you come to a grassy plateau cross it, eastwards, and you will find a pathway leading into woodland. Carry on along the line of the ridge. Shortly after passing the top of a ski-lift, you will come to a place where paths cross at the Col de Queffaix.

**Col de Queffaix or la Crouaz**
1,521m

Leaving the pass, the GR first leads through undergrowth - the local waymarks are orange - then across the slope in a more open area. A stiff climb brings you up to a low saddle and the upper station of the Combet chair-lift. On your right, you can see the Tête des Fieux 1,772 metres high. Look out for the waymarking which may have been affected by engineering work on ski-lifts. Cross the ski slope, follow the access path to the top of the chair-lift downhill for about 50 metres, then take a pathway uphill on your right through green alders. Climb up to the ridge at 1,750 metres. To the south, there is a view of the Darbon valley. The path turns eastwards to the left, follows the ridge - there is a cross on a mound - and comes to a fresh hollow in the ground with a small cabin at 1,771

**1:20**

metres; this is the lower end of a grassy ridge leading up to the Pointe de Pelluaz, 1,910 metres high. Do not follow the ridge, but bear left, to the north east, on a path crossing the slope. The path takes you under a chair-lift and down to the Chalet Vert. There is a spring just above the chalet and on your left a path leading to Les Combes and Pré Richard. The GR leads down into the combe, then climbs steeply again, east north-eastwards, up to the ridge line. The local waymarking is red. Follow the left-hand side of the ridge to the north east - take care if the grass is wet. You are now on the boundary between the cantons of Abondance and Evian and will soon come to the Col de la Case d'Oche.

**Col de la Case d'Oche**
*1,812m*

0:15

Walk downhill north east to the left, to reach the lakes.

**Lacs d'Oche or Lacs de la Case**
*1,750m*
*(see map ref F)*
*Reeds and other aquatic plants are gradually taking over these lakes; you are in a vast ampitheatre, surrounded by majestic mountains; looking north from left to right, you can see La Dent d'Oche - 2,221 metres, Le Col de Planchamp d'Oche - 1,999 metres, Le Château d'Oche, 2,197 metres high, whose steep northern face has only rarely been conquered, the Portes d'Oche gap - 1,937 metres, the north face of Les Pointes de Darbon, 2,030 metres high, first climbed in 1944, the Col de la Case d'Oche, where you have just come from, La Pointe de Pelluaz, and so on.*

**Junction** The GR Balcon du Léman separates from the GR5 Alternative Route on the left and goes north-westwards towards the ruins of the old upper Chalet d'Oche and on to the alpine Chalets d'Oche at 1,630 metres.

It is possible to get to Novel - and thence Saint Gingolph - by following the GR Balcon du Léman as far as the Col de Neuva and there taking, either,
1. the GR to the west down into the Morge valley; or,
2. the Alternative Route to the north via La Montagne de Mémises.

**0:50**

**Detour** *1 hr 30 mins*
## REFUGE DE LA DENT D'OCHE
⌂ ✕

*2,113m*
*Magnificent views over Lake Geneva and the Alps, with exceptional sunrises and sunsets; the summit of La Dent d'Oche, 2,221 metres high, is 15 minutes' walk from the refuge, providing a marvellous view 1,800 metres over the lake; the north face, with a sheer drop of 350 metres, was finally conquered in 1925.*

**Detour** Follow the path, in a north-westerly direction, past the Chalets d'Oche and, shortly before you come to the Col de Rebollion, turn north east towards La Dent d'Oche.

The GR5 skirts the 2 lakes, one of which is covered with weed, climbs eastwards up the left-hand of the combe, from where you have a good view of the gap in the face of Les Pointes de Darbon, and brings you to the Col des Portes d'Oche.

**Col des Portes d'Oche**
*1,937m*
*The col is a deep cleft between Les Pointes de Darbon - 2,030 metres - on the right and the Roc du Château d'Oche - 2,197 metres - on the left.*

Do not follow the path which goes straight down to the lake, but cut across the side of an area of scree to the left, from where you overlook the Lac de Darbon. There is a fine view south-eastwards over Les Dents-du-Midi and the Mont-Blanc massif as a whole. The GR leads on to the Col de Planchamp or Col de Pavis, 1,994 metres high, then makes its way down to the north west through alpine pastures. Below the Chauffes-Floras rocks, it reaches the junction with the GR5.

**0:45**

**Junction**
*1,873m*
*(see map ref 4)*

The Alternative GR5 joins the GR5 itself coming from Saint-Gingolph to the north.

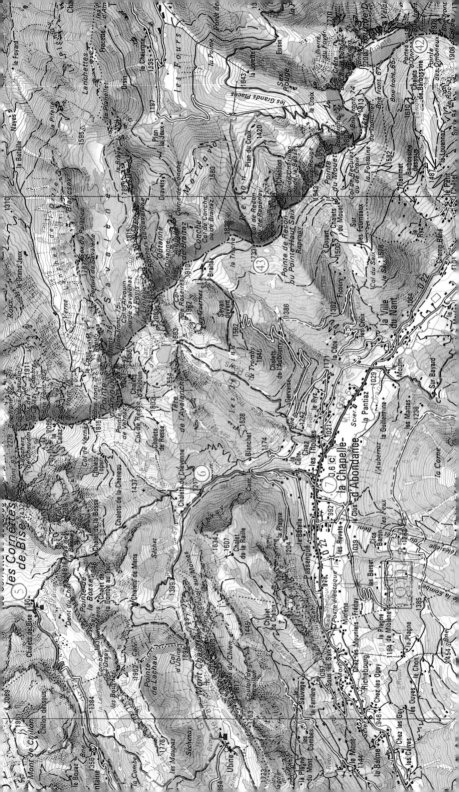

## Saint-Gingolph

Built on a strategic site between the shores of Lake Geneva and a rugged mountain massif, the village has for centuries experienced a very chequered history, owing to its position straddling the frontier between France and Switzerland. One local peculiarity is la Bourgeoisie, a social and civic structure which is more historical than economic, dating back to the Middle Ages. It was only later, around 1629, that the Gingolais began to buy meadows and woodland for themselves. Today the Bourgeoisie, a private association consisting of 19 families with separate councils on either side of the frontier, manages three quarters of the land and property within the area of the commune. The church, presbytery - the local priest is automatically a bourgeois - and a large part of the cemetery also form part of the Bourgeoisie's domain, as does the Château de Riedmaten, now the mairie of the Swiss part of Saint Gingolph, with a museum well worth a visit. Church, cemetery and village band, the Echo of the 2 Republics, are shared by the Swiss and French parts of the village.

The actual frontier is the Morge stream. The status of the land on either bank was decided by a convention of 1881 defining the frontier between Mont-Dolent in the Mont-Blanc massif and Lake Geneva, and referring back to the treaty of peace and friendship concluded at Thonon in 1569. On the French side private property runs right down to the edge of the public waterway, whereas on the Swiss side the canton of Valais has rights over the land along the river, and building is forbidden within 2 metres of the bank, so as not to hinder customs officers in the performance of their duties.

Many other anecdotes might be told about the closely interwoven relationship between the twin villages of Saint-Gingolph and their 725 inhabitants.

### SAINT-GINGOLPH

⌂ ⌂ ▲ 🚉 🚌

*386m*

*(see map ref 1)*

*The parish church of Novel stood on this site, until it was swept away by a huge landslide; on the gravestones you will find the names of as many as 10 generations of some families; there is also the unusual tomb of Gabon, the legendary village trumpeter, who recently died.*

**1:30**

The Haute-Savoie section of the GR5 starts just outside the village, on the Evian side, under the railway bridge. At first it follows the D30 road to Novel, then a good track, the former road, which climbs and runs along the left bank of the Morge. After La Morta, it continues uphill and crosses the D30 to a small graveyard.

The GR now comes to the first houses of Novel.

### NOVEL

⌂ ✗ 🚉

*960m*

*(see map ref 2)*

**Junction** The GR Balcon du Léman which passes through Les Mémises joins the GR5 on the right.

*Just under 100 inhabitants, the Novellands, live in this 700-year-old village, which was completely destroyed by fire in 1924; it lies at the foot of Le Pic Blanchard, 1,545 metres high, and La Dent d'Oche, 2,222 metres, facing the magnificent cliffs of Le Grammont, 2,176 metres high, on the Swiss side; the church still has some vestiges of its past, such as the granite key-stones in the arches, dated 1763, 1800 and 1828.*

0:40

The GR follows the road in front of the Hotel Grammont, crosses it and makes for the old wash house. It climbs up through the village, then cuts across a number of hairpin bends in the road to the car park at La Planche.

**La Planche**
*1,160*
*(see map ref 3)*

**Junction** The GR Balcon de Léman coming from the Chalets d'Oche and the Col de Neuva joins the GR5 on the right.

The GR5 continues on up the road in a south-westerly direction. After 500 metres, take a pathway on your left, which crosses the Rasses stream and brings you to a crossways. The GR continues south, uphill to the left, running along the side of the Vez ravine. The gradient increases to negotiate a rocky spur. The next landmark is the Chalets de Neutel at 1,750 metres, now renovated. The path goes on uphill to the south west - until it comes to the junction.

0:20

**Junction**
*(see map ref 4)*

The GR5 Alternative Route from Thonon-les-Bains joins the GR5.

**Warning** From the lie of the land, you would expect to continue south westwards, following the Alternative Route towards the Col de Planchamp, whereas the GR5 in fact gradually veers to the south, climbing to the Col de Bise.

0:30

**Col de Bise**
*1,215m*
*This is an important pass for travellers on foot, also known as the Col de Biémalet.*

Follow - **with care** - the path on the left, to the east, leading along ridges to La Tête de Charousse, 2,003 metres, and La Dent du Velan, 2,094 metres high on the Franco-Swiss border.

0:40

*There is a fine view of the Oche chain to the north*

The GR now zigzags steeply down through several hairpin bends into meadowland,

west and, to the south east,
Les Cornettes de Bise
2,432 metres high.

## CHALETS DE BISE
⌂ ✗

*1,502m*
*(see map ref 5)*
*The chalets lie at the foot of
Les Cornettes de Bise, at
the end of the road from
Vacheresse; the shepherds
will supply you with dairy
products; walkers who are
not in a hurry are
recommended to break
their journey here, and
spend a day exploring Les
Cornettes de Bise, a fine
walk with magnificent views
and the chance of seeing
alpine ibex.*

0::50

### Pas de la Bosse
*1,816m*
*Views of Les Dents-du-Midi
and Le Grand Combin
4,314 metres high.*

0:40

### Pont des Chalets de Chevenne
*1,217m*
*(see map ref 6)*

1:40

## LA CHAPELLE d'ABONDANCE
⌂ ⌂ Å ⚓

*1,021M*
*(see map ref 7)*
*Formerly known as La
Chapelle des Frasses, the
village is beautifully situated
in the heart of the
Abondance valley: the
villagers, known as the
Chapellans, have created a
friendly and charming
resort; there are 2 tourist
seasons; in winter, visitors*

1:50

crossing a number of streams on the way. It
reaches the Nant de Bise stream and follows
its right bank down to the Chalets de Bise.

**Junction** The GR5 joins a path linking up with
the local GR Portes du Soleil and leaving the
chalets continues eastwards, through hairpin
bends on up to the Pas de la Bosse.

The GR5 makes its way down to the Chalets
de la Bosse and the Chalets de la Cheneau.
The path runs alongside a wood, cuts through
it and crosses the Chevenne stream. It turns
right, to the south and joins the road near the
bridge.

The GR5, joined by the Local GR Portes du
Soleil, turns left, to the south, and follows the
Chevenne stream, to La Chapelle
d'Abondance.

**Junction** At La Chapelle d'Abondance the local
GR Tour des Portes du Soleil" leaves the GR5
and heads north east towards the Lac d'Arvouin.

From La Chapelle d'Abondance the GR5 follows
the D22 road south east towards Châtel.

**Warning** Walkers should keep a sharp look
out for the traffic on this very busy road. The
La Chapelle commune is currently trying to
establish a new route to enable walkers to
escape the motor traffic.

On leaving the hamlet of La Pantiaz, at 1,029
metres, turn right immediately after a bridge

*come for alpine skiing in the vast Portes du Soleil area and cross-country skiing over the 60-70 km of ski trails; in summer, they come to walk and explore the valley.*

and go down to cross the River Dranse. A little further on, take the footpath climbing up southwards through low growth along the Mattes stream and its waterfalls, as far as the chalet of Sur Bayard.

## The Abondance Valley

The action of glaciers and their melt-waters over thousands of years has created a valley now rich in pastoral activity, architecture, historical associations and natural beauty. As you walk, take time to enjoy the varied sights, sounds, smells and tastes it has to offer, for example:

*Abondance abbey*, 5 km from the village, has a cloister built between 1331 and 1356, frescoes unlike any others in the Alps - and abbey church dating from 1820, with magnificent vaulting spanning 19 metres where the transept crosses the nave. There is also a museum housing the abbey treasures.

*Onion-dome bell towers.* The one at La Chapelle d'Abondance is among the finest. Some people consider that onion domes indicate oriental influence, brought back in this case by the crusaders. Others believe Napoleon's soldiers were responsible for introducing them. Two more probable theories are that people from Savoy who emigrated from the high valleys to Switzerland, Italy and Bavaria, and as far as Vienna, brought the oriental forms with them when they returned, or even more likely, that the bell towers were the work of Piedmontese and Tuscan craftsmen, who moved from village to village and eventually reached these valleys.

*Chalet architecture.* The valley is fortunate in having its own style of chalet, some bearing some resemblance to those of the Valais and even the more distant Tyrol, but still quite distinct. The house backs onto the mountain side, with a big drop in level between the main façade and hay loft.

The part for human habitation always faces south, with unusual balconies running from one side to the other, their finely carved balustrades of reddish spruce wood darkened by constant exposure to the sun. From the small vegetable garden there is direct access to cellars in the stone foundations; on the eastern side is a water trough, constantly replenished by running water; and there are two doors, one to the living quarters, the other to the stable.

The part backing on to the mountain side has a large double door, to give easy access for sledges laden with hay. On the western side of the building, projecting eaves keep off the rain and snow.

The living area is reached by steps up from the garden or via internal stairways, very useful in winter for getting from the barn to the stable or the living quarters. Notice, too, the slope of the roof, its shingle or slate tiling, and the chimney, known to locals as the bourne.

*Granaries.* These are simple chalets, on one or two levels, sited 50 or 60 paces away from the main dwelling as a precaution in case of fire. Here people kept not only corn, oats, honey and local brandy, but also their valuables and carefully concealed caches of money. The massive wooden door locks with a huge key, and sometimes a keyhole cover to keep out the mice. The stone base of the granary keeps it off the ground.

*The abondancières*: fine, fat cows of the Abondance breed, also known as lunettes because they have brown and red-flecked rings, like spectacles, around their eyes. Excellent milkers, they are sturdy and firm of foot on the mountain sides. In late May or early June they are driven up to the high alpine pastures, coming down to the valley again in early October. Each herd is led by its queen, a cow who has established her dominance over her sisters. The herdsman knows each of his animals by the sound of the bell round her neck: in a mist he can locate each cow, and easily find them if they linger in woodland. There are two kinds of cowbell. Those made of bronze, the campàgnnes, which hang from a broad collar and may be up to 100 years old, engraved with the name of their founder, and also with the sign of the cross or the Virgin Mary for protection; and those of iron, the potè, which are round in shape, with a duller sound. In these valleys, cowbells have the same significance as clocks or pieces of furniture for families in other parts of the world; they are heirlooms to be lovingly handed down from generation to generation.

On you way through the valley look out too for local crafts, or the fruitière, the local dairy where Abondance cheese is made.

*From Following the Dranse d'Abondance by Bruno Gillet*

---

**Sur Bayard**
*1,219m*

Take the footpath which runs east, on the level, and after 300 metres climbs up by hairpin bends through woodland to join a forest track. Follow this to the left for a few metres, then carry on along a path going south, down the Vallon de la Guerliaz, to the recently renovated Chalet des Crottes at 1,529 metres. Ruins of the old farm are lower down the valley. The GR takes the path running under the high tension electric power line and into a little valley that leads to a huge cirque, dominated on the west by the 2,010 metres high Pointe des Mattes and further on by the Mont de Grange, 2,432 metres high, and then to the Chalet de la Torrens, at 1,738 metres.

2:30

*Milk may be available at the chalet.*

Take the track behind the chalet, climbing up south west in a combe, and then over some very rough scree, to reach the Col des Mattes.

**Le Col des Mattes**
*1,930m*

From the Col, go down southwards to the Chalet des Mattes and on to the Chalets du Pron at 1,741 metres. The GR carries on south through several bends, then runs along on the level, westwards, crossing first the Etrye stream and then the Coincon, and reaches the Chalet de L'Etrye.

0:50

**0:30**

### Chalet de L'Etrye
*1,694m*
*Renovated summer farm.*
*GTA sign gives altitude as*
*1,670 metres.*

### Crête de Coincon
*1,840m*
**Detour** *2 hrs*
### Le Mont de Grange
*2,432m*
*Protected by a conservation order and designated as a game reserve, Le Mont de Grange, highest peak in the Savoyard Chablais, is a magnificent pyramid of limestone with traces of siliceous grit, with very varied landscape ranging from beech woods through fir and spruce forest, alder coppice, high pastures, to stretches of rock and grassland, at the different sub-alpine and alpine levels; fauna rich in certain species, notably chamois and mouflon, and a diverse and flourishing alpine flora, both protected from the 1,100 metres level upwards to the summit; Triangulation point.*

**1:00**

### Sharp bend
*1,664m*
**Detour** *30 mins*
### PLAINE DRANSE GÎTE D'ÉTAPE
⌂ ✗
*Chapel dedicated to the Virgin, at the foot of a rock.*

**0:15**

Follow a broad track south-westwards, curving through 4 bends around the south-east shoulder of the Crête de Coincon.

**Detour** Walkers will find a path going to the right, west north west, up the slopes and then over grassland. Running along the Coincon ridge it passes the 2,004 metres marker, then climbs steeply towards a first grassy saddle. Turning directly north on a well maintained track it reaches the first rocks, on the approach to the summit and its wide panoramic views. Follow the same route down again.

From the Coincon ridge you come to the Chalets de Lenlevay at 1,745 metres, then to a very broad col with GTA sign saying 1,740 metres, altitude marker 1,733 metres. Ignore a track to the right which leads to the Chalets du Jouly, and continue along a track going south west and then bearing south east on the level for 1.8 kilometres. Follow this track through the Forêt des Rubis till you come to a very sharp bend.

**Detour** Keeping to the track, head eastwards, passing Les Grands Plans at 1,664 metres, and carry on through wide bends to join the Châtel-Bassachau road. Follow this to the left, passing La Mouille Ronde before reaching the large hamlet of Plaine Dranse and its cable-lift stations.

At the sharp bend, the GR5 leaves the track and climbs southwards on a path through a very marshy area to reach the Col de Bassachaux.

## COL DE BASSACHAUX
⌂ 🚟
*1,778m*
*Between La Pointe de la
Gouille Rose, or Pointe de
Lens, 1,827 metres high,
and the Tête de Lindaret,
1,950 metres, at the
provisional terminus of the
new Les Lindarets - Châtel
road; Oratory; By going
down the road, eastwards,
on the châtel side, one can
reach the Plaine Dranse gîte
in about 30 minutes.*

**1:35**

### Col de Chésery
*1,963m to 2,024m
On the Franco-Swiss
frontier, between Haute-
Savoie and Valais. Note that
the Swiss section of the
GR5 is mostly waymarked
with the Swiss mountain
footpath marks, which are
white-red-white.*

**0:15**

## REFUGE DE CHÉSERY
## OR DU LAC VERT
⌂

**0:35**

### Col des Portes de
### l'Hiver, or Portes du
### Lac Vert
*2,157m
Dominated on the west by
La Pointe de Mossetaz, or
Mossette, 2,284 metres,
and its cable lift;
exceptional views over the
high pastures - and in the
winter the extensive ski
slopes - of Champéry, and
over the Dents-du-Midi,
3,527 metres, the rounded
snowy dome of Le Grand
Mont Ruan, 3,040 metres,
the Dents Blanches, 2,711
metres, and the Tête de
Bossetan, 2,406 metres.*

**0:05**

From the col the GR heads south-eastwards, on the level, passing below the Tête de Lindaret and the Crête de Rochassons, 1,931 metres, with views to the west over the Lac de Montrion, and comes to a little chalet.

Ignore the path going off right, to Les Lindarets, and continue along the flank, south-westwards, across huge alpine pastures, with a view to the south of the Pointe de Vorlaz, 2,346 metres, and Les Hauts-Forts, 2,466 metres. Carry on over some stony patches to reach the Col de Chésery.

At the frontier post the GR5 continues eastwards, passes above the Customs hut, and descends to the Refuge de Chésery.

Following around the northern and north-eastern banks of the Lake, the GR climbs up to the Col des Portes de l'Hiver.

From the Col des Portes de l'Hiver descend southwards until you come to a fork.

**Road Fork**

0:25

**CHAUX-PALIN,**
*or Champalin*
⌂ ✕
*1,843m*
*(see map ref 8)*
**Detour** *20 mins*
**LES CROSETS**
1:20
Ⓗ ⌂ ⬛
**Detour** *30 mins*
**CRÊTE BORNET**
⌂ ✕
**Detour** *30 mins*
**Champéry cable-car station**
*Departure point for Tour des Dents-du-Midi*

The local GR Tour des Portes du Soleil joins the GR5; the GR5 and the local GR share the same route as far as a crossroads not far from the Chalets de Fréterolle.

The 2 GRs carry on together to reach the Chalets de Chaux-Palin.

From Chaux-Palin the GR5 heads south, passes the foot of the Pointe de Chavanette, 2,216 metres, and, running along the base of the frontier ridges, reaches the Chalets du Pas, at 1,856 metres, then the Chalets de la Pisaz, and finally those of Poyat.

Alpine flora, Rhododendrons

43

**Poyat**
*1,646m*
*Farm chalets in alpine
pastures below the Pointe
de Fornet, 2,298 metres
and the Pointe de la
Léchère, 2,174 metres. Fine
views over Les Creuses
and the Val d'Illiez.*

0:40

The path drops a little to reach the track coming from Champéry, then climbs through a whole series of hairpin bends, amidst banks of rhododendrons - in flower during July and August - to the Col de Coux.

**Col de Coux**
*1,920m*
*(see map ref 9)*
*On the French-Swiss frontier
between Le Vanet, 2,136
metres, and La Berte, 1,992
metres; Swiss ornithological
station; windpump.*
**Detour** *15 mins*
**La Berte**

0:30

*Wide views, with the Col de
la Golèse to the south west,
the Pointe d'Angolon, 2,090
metres and the Pointe de
Nyon, 2,019 metres, to the
west, as well as the Pré-
Alps of Chablais and farther
away to the south west, La
Pointe Percée and Les
Aravis.*

**Junction** The Local GR Tour des Dents-du-Midi joins the GR5; the 2 GRs share the same route as far as the Col de la Golèse.

**Detour** Follow a grassy ridge running south till you reach the summit of La Berte.

The GRs follow the well marked path descending first over grassland and then among alders, where it becomes narrower. You come to a fine spruce forest, and after a few hairpin bends arrive at a crossroads.

**Crossroads**
*1,600m*
*(see map ref 10)*

**Detour** *20 mins*
**LES MINES D'OR**
⌂ ✗

The local GR Tour des Portes du Soleil leaves the GR5, leading westwards down the valley towards Morzine.

**Detour** Turn right at the crossroads and follow the local GR down past the Chalets de Fréterolle to the gâte and refuge at Les Mines d'Or.

From the crossroads follow a track running down through the forest to a car park at the terminus of the Morzine - Le Charny tarmac road. The GR crosses the Nant - notice the yellow waymarks of the route leading to the Pas de la Latte - then goes downhill across a huge grassy combe. At the bottom, the footpath runs through bushes for a short way, then comes out into a broad valley, and curves around on its flank with the cliffs of the Terres Maudites above on the left. Lower down, to the north

1:20

west, one can glimpse the farm buildings of Chardonnière. After passing through more forest, the path joins a road near the Chalet de Bonnevalette.

**Chalet de Bonnevalette**
*1,568m*
**Detour** *10 mins*
**VIGNY**
△ ✕
0:40
*Take the path going off to the right, past the chalets, to the refuges at Vigny.*

Where the paths diverge, the GR5 turns south and climbs up to the Col de la Golèse.

**Col de la Golèse**
*1,569m*
*(see map ref 11)*
*Narrow pass at the foot of the broken rocky escarpments of the Pointe de la Golèse, 1,835 metres. Springs.*
0:50

**Junction**

The local GR Tour des Dents-du-Midi leaves the GR5 and heads eastwards.

**Detour** *30 mins*
**REFUGE TORNAY**
△ ✕
*1,763m*

**Detour** From the Col de la Golèse an un-waymarked local GR path heads left, south east, to the refuge. On leaving Tornay, walkers can rejoin the GR5 by following the path going south west through the Forêt de Bossetan or Bostan to reach a junction at 1,096 metres, after about 2 hours walking time.

---

**Col de la Golèse**
The Col de la Golèse is situated on an important line of route for migratory birds. Each autumn more than a thousand birds are netted, ringed and recorded here by ornithologists. Out of the 120,000 or so ringed over a 25 year period, only 3,000 have been netted again. Nevertheless, the scientists have been able to draw some interesting conclusions, such as the cyclic nature of the migration of certain species. Coal tits, for example, come through La Golèse every 2 years on their way to Italy, Spain, and even Egypt. Blue tits, on the other hand, come through every year; one blue tit was recaptured every year for 7 years. A siskin from Lithuania on the Baltic Sea and another from Leningrad in the USSR, and coal tits from Poland, have been recorded at the Col. Other researchers here are studying migratory insects, like such diptera as flies, mosquitoes and midges.

**0:05**

The GR5 now enters the valley of the Giffre. Follow the motor road down to the right, towards Chavonnes, at 1,269 metres. At the chalets, carry on down, to the south east, and then eastwards, passing the chalets of Les Bervalles at 1,154 metres, and then at a sharp bend in the road you come to a junction.

The local GR rejoins the GR5.

The GR5 continues along the road to Les Allamands.

**Les Allamands**
*1,028m*
*(see map ref 12)*
*Farming village - perhaps named after the Alamani, a Germanic tribe vanquished in the 5th century by the Frankish King Clovis; Chapel.*

**0:30**

The GR5 continues along the road, southwards, to a wayside Calvary, where the local GR Tour des Dents-du-Midi comes in from the Refuge de Folly, and then after several hairpin bends reaches Le Pied du Crêt at 889 metres. Take the footpath eastwards across the Grand-Pré and then a path to the right as far as a crossroads.

**Crossroads**
*(see map ref 13)*

**Junction** of the GR5 with the local GR Tour des Dents-du-Midi.

**Detour** *2 hrs*
**REFUGE DE FOLLY**
⌂
*1,558m*
*Close by is the Ermoy cave, a designated site.*
*Follow the steep footpath running up beside the Les Landes stream.*

**0:40**

The GR5 takes a well marked path through a cutting, crosses the Les Landes stream and follows the left bank to the hamlet of Le Chevreret at 748 metres, then carries on down to Les Moulins and the town of Samoëns.

**SAMOËNS**
🏠 ⌂ 🏕 🍴 🍷 🚃 🚌 🅱
*703m*
*(see map ref 14)*

**Junction** Departure point of GR96 going towards Lac d'Annecy; the GR96 shares the GR5 route as far as Pont de Nant, GR96 Alternative Route via Le Désert de Platé shares it as far as Les Pleureuses; GR5 also shares route here with the European footpath E2 on which Samoëns is a staging point.

The GR5 leaves Samoëns by way of the hamlet of Les Moulins. From there, walkers have a choice of two ways to reach the hamlet of Perret.

## Samoëns

Tucked away at the foot of the 2,200 metres Montagne de Criou, Samoëns is a very pleasant resort, both for summer sports - swimming, riding, free flying, rafting, fishing, archery, rifle-shooting, tennis, volley-ball, climbing and walking - and for winter sports. Samoëns forms an integral part of the Grand Massif ski station, which has 250 kilometres of ski runs, 71 cable lifts, and more than 71 kilometres of cross-country ski routes.

The town certainly welcomes visitors, priding itself on an annual influx of 15,000 holidaymakers to compare with its population of rather less than 2,000 inhabitants. The only holiday resort designated as being of artistic and historical interest by the National Register of Historic Monuments, Samoëns is rich in history. Its Place du Gros-Tilleul - Great Lime-Tree Square - dating from 1438 - is ringed with very ancient monuments that witness to the skill of Samoëns builders, who from the 16th century on were highly sought after, going off to Savoy, to other parts of France, and even further afield, to Poland, Louisiana ... and building churches, castles, fortifications, canals ....

Close to the church, the Jaysinia alpine botanic garden - founded by a local inhabitant, Madame Marie-Lousie Cognacq Jay who also started La Samaritaine in Paris - contains in its 3 hectares or so of ground more than 4,500 mountain plant species from all 5 continents.

On the business side, the town is active throughout the year, with more than 100 shops and other services, 25 hotels, and an important Wednesday market.

1:10

1. The old route, now tarmac but not very busy, which runs first towards Vallon-d'en-Bas, then up to Vallon-d'en-Haut, where there are fine old Savoyard houses, to Sougey and, a bit farther on, Le Perret, where it joins the new route.

2. The new route which keeps to the left bank of the Clévieux stream, leaves Les Moulins by a small road running south, crosses the D907 and follows a footpath into the Samoëns communal forest, passing close to the Nant d'Ant waterfall which is a designated site. Near to the confluence of the Clévieux and Giffre streams the GRs run along the protective dyke on the left bank and then take a track following the course of the river. They come out on the D907 road again shortly before the hamlet that has given its name to the Pont-Perret.

**PONT-PERRET**

726m
*Oratory dated 1826.*

Turn right across the bridge over the Giffre, and on to a small road going up to the hamlet of Les Faix. From there continue on a broad track running on the level to reach the forest.

**Detour** *5 mins*

**Chapelle Notre-Dame des Graces**

*Cool and refreshing spot overlooking the Giffre, second largest mountain stream in Haute-Savoie, after the Arve, with a flow of 49 cubic feet per second.*

0:20

**Footbridge over the Giffre**

*735m*

*Metal construction at the foot of Les Tines gorges; designated site.*

*This section of the path was carved out by the tongue of the glacier which originally gave birth to the Giffre; a remarkable site, with great cauldrons in the limestone hollowed out by the water over thousands of years.*

0:15

**Head of the gorges**

*850m*

0:15

**Detour** *30 mins*

**SIXT-FER-À-CHEVAL**

*Founded in 1144 by Ponce de Faucigny who built an abbey here - its church and some buildings now a hotel still remain; Sixt massif, characterised by altitudes ranging from 756 to 3,096 metres and varied terrain, includes forests, alpine pasturelands and mineral resources - iron ores - all fully exploited by its people; Lime tree in the town is a designated site.*

**Detour** *4 hours*

**Cirque du Fer-à-Cheval**

**Detour** Turn left off the path to reach the chapel.

The path then slopes down on to a huge meadow, which it crosses diagonally to reach a footbridge over the Giffre.

Do not cross the footbridge, but take a path to the right, above two ruined farm buildings, which climbs through the forest and then through a narrow gorge along the old bed of the Giffre. Three of the steeper rocky stretches are equipped with ladders.

Carry on to the upper end of the gorges.

At the head of the gorges, the GRs take a footpath to the right, winding upwards along the base of the cliffs through a low growth of beech and spruce. Another ladder takes you up to a ledge with a view over the whole of the Sixt basin. The path then follows a series of bends down a rocky slope, and across a meadow to three old chalets, reaching the Giffre-Haut stream and then at the Fonds stream, the Pont des Nants.

**Detour** At the head of the gorges, take a footpath to the left, running down to the gorge of Les Tines itself and crossing it by an impressive bridge which takes you on to the D907, close to a black marble quarry. Follow the road to the right for 50 metres, and there turn on to a footpath along the old railway line, now a public path. Follow this on into the village of Sixt.

**Detour** In summer the excursion to the cirque, 7 kilometres from Sixt, can be undertaken by

*955m*
*Striking panorama;*
*designated site.*

bus. Walkers can either follow the D907 heading north east, or take a route which leaves Maison Neuve, just south of Sixt, heading east to climb up through Lavoisière and then north east to Passy. From there, waymarked in yellow, it runs along the flank of the Montagne de Commune via the hamlets of Verduize at 1,329 metres, Les Mouillettes at 1,434 metres, the chalets and barns of Commune at 1,674 metres and finally after going down through the woods, Le Pelly at 930 metres.

## Pont des Nants
*768m*
*(see map ref 15)*

**Junction** Starting point of the GR96 Alternative route to Flaine via the Dèsert de Platé, a designated site; the regular GR96 leaves the GR5. The GR96 Alternative shares the GR5 route as far as the waterfalls of La Pleureuse. The regular GR96 continues along the road, climbing to Englème at 850 metres, the Chalets de Gers at 1,544 metres and the Col Pelouse at 2,227 metres; then comes down again to Flaine at 1,650 metres where its Alternative route via the Désert de Platé rejoins it.

0:30
or
0:35

The GR5 and GR96 Alternative cross the Pont des Nants. Just beyond the bridge walkers have a choice of 2 possible routes to the Pont de Salles:
1. Waymarked route, 30 minutes' walking time. Just beyond the Pont des Nants turn right and up along the right bank of the stream. Cross a footbridge to reach the Pont de Salles.
2. Unwaymarked route, 35 minutes' walking time. Go through Fay, with its old houses and chapel, dated 1641 and 1869. At Maison Neuve follow the D29 to the right as far as Salvigny at 850 metres, a designated site. Go through the village and on along the road to the Pont de Salles.

## PONT DE SALLES
**Ⱥ**
*850m*

0:20

Cross the stream and follow the road for a few metres. Then take a track going up to the left through the forest. On the right, beside the stream is a camp site which welcomes walkers. After crossing a stream by a ford just below the road bridge, continue along the road to the Le Rouget waterfall.

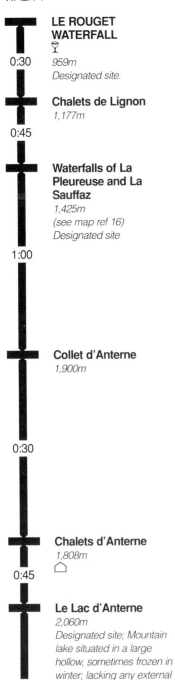

**LE ROUGET WATERFALL**
☿
0:30 *959m*
*Designated site.*

**Chalets de Lignon**
*1,177m*
0:45

**Waterfalls of La Pleureuse and La Sauffaz**
*1,425m*
*(see map ref 16)*
*Designated site*
1:00

**Collet d'Anterne**
*1,900m*
0:30

**Chalets d'Anterne**
*1,808m*
⌂
0:45

**Le Lac d'Anterne**
*2,060m*
*Designated site; Mountain lake situated in a large hollow, sometimes frozen in winter; lacking any external*

Cutting across the hairpin bends of the road, the GRs continue on up, passing the Chalets du Fardelay at 1,039 metres, and then climbing as far as the Chalets du Lignon.

The GRs run closer to the Salles stream, carry on climbing through the forest and after a short bend, with a view over the falls, reach the waterfalls of La Pleureuse.

**Junction** The GR96 Alternative route leaves the GR5.

The GR96 Alternative continues climbing south-westwards to the Chalets de Salles, and then the Refuge du Platé. From there you can either turn north west to rejoin the GR96 at Flaine, or go south, down to the Plateau d'Assy.

At the level of the waterfalls the GR5 forks back to the left from the junction, heading north east, and climbs along the north flank of the Pointe de Salles to the Collet d'Anterne.

The GR descends a little, crosses the Anterne stream at 1,748 metres, and reaches the rather marshy alpine pasture of Anterne.

**Warning** At this stage the waymarking is sometimes hard to see. Take your bearing on the chalets ahead, or in case of fog, follow the right bank of the stream, and then that of the first streamlet you come to.

The GR passes some sheep pens and then comes to a level plateau and the Chalets d'Anterne.

The GR continues southwards, crosses the Anterne stream and a number of streamlets, and runs along beside the east bank of the Lac d'Anterne.

From the lake the GR heads south over a stretch where you may often find snow still lying, even at the end of summer, hidden away in some of the combes. The path climbs on beside a little stream to reach the Col d'Anterne.

**0:45**

*outlet its waters drain through a fissure in the limestone; Immediately above it, notice the precipitous and sharply eroded rocks of the Tête à l'Ane.*

### Col d'Anterne
*2,257m*
*Broad saddle marked by a wooden cross. Panoramic view of the Mont-Blanc range filling the horizon, with the Aiguilles Rouges in the foreground. On the right the Rochers des Fiz form 2 sides of a veritable natural fortress, with the Pointe d'Anterne at 2,733 metres like a watch tower at its corner.*

The GR5 descends south-westwards to a junction.

**0:15**

### Junction

The GR5 is joined by the local GR 'Tour du Pays du Mont-Blanc'. This local GR runs south west to Servoz; westwards to the Plateau d'Assy; north-eastwards it makes a tour of the Aiguilles Rouges; here and there it shares a route with the GR5.

From the junction the GR5 turns left, north-eastwards, in a hairpin bend to reach the Cantine-Refuge de Moëde.

**0:15**

### CANTINE-REFUGE DE MOËDE OR D'ANTERNE
△ Å ▭
*1,995m*
*(see map ref 17)*
*Overlooks the Lac du Laouchet and, farther off, the Lac de Pormenaz.*

The local GR Tour du Pays du Mont-Blanc continues eastwards and then north-eastwards towards the Aiguilles Rouges massif. The GR5 and the local GR Tour du Pays du Mont-Blanc Alternative share the same route as far as Les Houches. From the Cantine-Refuge at Moëde the GR5 takes the footpath heading south east, passing the Chalets de Moëde and running along the left bank of the Moëde stream. As you approach the Tête de Jeubont, 1,712 metres, leave the stream and bear left, down to the Pont d'Arlevé.

**0:35**

### Pont d'Arlevé

*1,597m*

*Bridge over the Doise or Diosaz; lower down, the stream runs through deep gorges it has carved on its way to join the Arve near Servoz. The bridge is removed each autumn, and replaced at the start of summer.*

**0:45**

After the bridge, the GR5 turns south, climbs up again, runs along below the Aiguilles Rouges, and after crossing a number of streamlets coming down from the Lacs Noirs or Lac Cornu, reaches the ruins of the Chalets d'Arlevé.

### Chalets d'Arlevé

*1,865m*

*Very ancient alpine pasture: documents relating to its sale in the 17th century refer to initial title deeds dating from 1443.*

**1:30**

The GR continues climbing south-eastwards, passes between La Montagne de la Coquille and the Pointe des Vioz, 2,451 metres high, and then by a series of hairpin bends up through the rocks, reaches the Col du Brévent.

### Col du Brévent

*2,368m*

*(see map ref 18)*

*Magnificent panorama of the whole Mont-Blanc range and the Chamonix valley; in the opposite direction one can see the Rochers des Fiz with the Col d'Anterne on the right.*

**Junction** The GR Tour du Mont-Blanc joins the GR5; these 2 GRs share the same route as far as the refuge at the Col de la Croix du Bonhomme. The stretch known as Le Balcon du Mont-Blanc, and the whole Mont-Blanc massif are a part of designated areas.

From the Col du Brévent the GR5 and GRTMB head south west along the northern slopes of Le Brévent, where there are views over the Diose valley with the Rochers des Fiz on the horizon, and often patches of snow still lying in summer, then climb round southwards to the summit.

**Detour** *45 mins*
### PLANPRAZ CABLE-CARSTATION

⌂ ⛴

**1:00**

*2,000m*

*Intermediate stop on the Chamonix-Le Brévent cable lift. Several local GR footpaths lead down to Chamonix via Les Chablettes, about 1 hour 30 minutes' walking time. To reach Planpraz follow the GRTMB route down south-eastwards, through some sharp bends.*

### Summit of Brévent

*2,526m*

The path goes down over scree with beautiful views over the Lac du Brévent below, then

*An easy summit to reach, Brévent is the best viewpoint for Mont-Blanc, from which one can see the whole development of the big Bossons and Taconna glaciers, as well as the climbing routes up to the highest summit in Europe; Orientation table; Upper terminal of cable-cars from Chamonix. New cable lift installed 1988.*

**0:40**

follows the south west spur of Brévent, where there are further views of the Mont-Blanc range.

Ignore a path on the right going to Aiguillette des Houches, just before you arrive at Bellachat.

The GR descends rapidly through a series of bends, cuts across the Vouillouds ravine and runs through a magnificent conifer forest. After passing the hamlet of Merlet, cross the La Pra ravine and a few metres farther on turn sharp left, out of the forest, and continue along the fence of the Merlet animal reserve.

**BELLACHAT**
⌂ ✕

*2,151m*
**Detour** *2 hrs 30 mins*
**CHAMONIX-MONT-BLANC**
⌂ ⌂ 🅰 ✕ 🍷 ⛟ ⛴
🚃 🚌

**0:45**

*1,010m*
*Cable lift terminus.*
*From Bellachat take the footpath going down eastwards, passing Plan-Lachat.*

---

**Glacier des Bossons**

Facing them, walkers will marvel at the glacier des Bossons, the biggest ice-fall in Europe: With 3,600 metres difference in altitude between its upper and lower limits, on a 45 degree slope, a surface length of 8 kilometres, and area around 1000 hectares, it drains the huge mass of ice from the west and north faces of Mont-Blanc, almost to the bottom of the valley.

This glacier attracts attention because it reaches down into inhabited areas, emerging from the inanimate frozen heights to end by behaving like a bulldozer, actually shifting rocks and knocking down trees. For thirty years now, the glaciers have been growing again, and the Glacier des Bossons is the prime example of this phenomenon. Its tongue has advanced 300 metres in 30 years and it has gained some ground at the top as well.

The Glacier des Bossons is also silent witness to the major catastrophes whose relics it carries with it. For example, in 1978 its tongue disgorged a mail bag from the Indian plane, the Malabar Princess, which crashed near the Mont-Blanc summit on 3 November 1950. And the bodies of climbers belonging to the Hamel expedition, who fell near the summit of Mont-Blanc in 1820, were found 40 years later and 3,600 metres lower down. (Quoted from Jean-Paul Roudier's Dauphiné Libéré).

## MERLET
⌂
*1,562m*

**Detour** *30 mins*
**Chalet-Hôtel de l'Aiguillette**

0:30

**Statue du Christ-Roi**
*1,268m*
*Concrete statue of Christ the King, work of the sculptor Serraz, 17 metres high, set on a 6 metres high plinth which houses a chapel.*

0:30

## LES HOUCHES
⌂ ⚕ ✕ ♈ ⚏ ⚏ ⚏ ⑫
*1,008m*
*(see map ref 19)*
*A pleasant village, long and narrow at the foot of l'Aiguille du Goûter, where Mont-Blanc country starts; Its church has a strange bulbous steeple, and an 18th century retable. The viaduct of Saint-Marie, 52 metres high and gorges of La Diose near Servoz, are within reach. Museum of rural and mountain life.*

**Detour** To reach the hotel, skirt round the reserve and take a footpath leading towards the Plan de la Cry-Coupeau, at first running along the mountain side and then becoming quite steep and passing below Le Lac Noir. Do not take any of the tracks to the right.

The GR then takes the gravel road around the park, leaving it before long and taking a path through the forest. Look out for waymarks painted on trees by the Forests Department, a wide white line with thin red lines in the middle and at each end. The path winds down through hairpin bends to reach the Christ-Roi statue.

The path continues down, leaves the forest and reaches a kind of esplanade where you immediately turn left on to a path going straight down and cutting across three bends in the tarmac road that goes up to Coupeau. The path reaches the EDF dam on the River Arve, where you turn right, and after a short descent, reach the SNCF station at Les Houches.

Les Houches is the starting point of Walk 2 'The Tour du Mont-Blanc'. Walk 1 and Walk 2 follow the same route as far as Les Chapieux.

# WALK 2

## The Tour du Mont-Blanc

T he famous guide and writer Roger Frison Roche, from Chamonix, author of many
works on the subject of mountains - Premier de cordée, La Grande Crevasse,
etc. - has put together in the two volumes of 'Les Montagnes de la terre', published
by Flammarion, the results of ten years of documentation, travels and researches
which make his book the complete Mountain Encyclopaedia everyone has been
waiting for. We have reproduced in this book part of the chapter dedicated to the
central crystalline massifs of Mont-Blanc and les Aiguilles Rouges, giving prospective
walkers a picture of the massif which you will see in reality when you follow the route
of the Tour de Mont-Blanc.

No-one could describe the Mont-Blanc range without recalling that it was at Chamonix,
then a simple community of farmers, stonecutters and chamois hunters living in this,
the most impressive glacial region in Europe that alpinism was born.

As the highest summit in the Alps, at 4,807 metres, Mont-Blanc inspired Horace-
Bénédict de Saussure to attempt climbing it in a scientific manner. The history of
alpinism describes the success of the Mont-Blanc guides and in particular the first
climb by Jacques Balmat and Dr Paccard, on 7 and 8 August 1786, a year before
de Saussure's own great historic climb. The famous Genevan had already been
through the Col du Géant, remaining for a long time at 3,345 metres and making
important observations of the mountain's climate and the effects of altitude, and also
studying the glaciers and rocks.

Chamonix-Mont-Blanc began to develop as a resort in the middle of the 19th
century, and today is the biggest mountain resort in the world. Home not only of the
Ecole Nationale de Ski et d'Alpinisme, where guides and skiers are trained, but also
of the famous 150 years old Compagnie des Guides. Chamonix has enjoyed further
development since the introduction of the Aiguille du Midi cable-cars to the Col du
Géant via the Mont-Blanc and Vallée Blanche terminals, which run high above the
Glacier du Géant. From the Col du Géant, the cable-car makes a speedy journey
between Pointe Helbronner and Entrèves, completing the high level route over the
Mont-Blanc range.

Without going into details of the four hundred summits described in specialised
guide books, let us just list the main ones, following the frontier ridge from Mont Dolent
where France, Italy and Switzerland meet, right along to the Cols de la Seigne and
du Bonhomme: l'Aiguille de Triolet, l'Aiguille de Leschaux, Grandes Jorasses - whose
north face, reaching 1,200 metres, includes some of the most famous climbing routes,
l'Aiguille du Géant - a veritable obelisk of granite, Tour Ronde, Mont Maudit, Mont-
Blanc, Dôme du Goûter; then at the Col du Dôme the Vallot refuge and observatory,
at 4,363 metres, are only exceeded in altitude by the Gnifetti hut on Mont Rose,
l'Aiguille de Bionnassay, Dôme de Miage, and l'Aiguille des Glaciers, the southernmost
peak of the range.

Only two of the glacial cols through this long range are passable without too much
difficulty: the Col du Géant and the Col de Miage. All the other routes present major

problems. The Col du Géant however seems to have been regularly used by the stonecutters. From this main range a number of noteworthy ridges extend northwards. Branching off from l'Aiguille de Triolet one can see the massif of l'Aiguille Verte, highest summit lying entirely within France, l'Aiguille du Dru, 3,754 metres, and Les Droites. From Mont Maudit, to the north, a long ridge running to Mont-Blanc du Tacul, continues on, after the glacial hollow of the Col du Midi, site of a cosmic rays observatory, via the Aiguilles de Chamonix range, a rock climbers' paradise beyond compare, with splendid granitic peaks consisting of fantastic rocky spires, pinnacles, pillars and needles.

From the Dôme du Goûter, a magnificent mountain entirely glacial in origin, a ridge slopes down to the Col de Voza, by the l'Aiguille du Goûter; the Dômes de Miage form a separate massif above Val Montjoie; and finally l'Aiguille des Glaciers carries on up to Mont Tondu, at the southern end of the range. Between these ridges and spurs are the most beautiful glaciers of the Alps.

The local fauna and flora, which are admirably protected and cared for, make the area around the massif a real nature park. There are many ibex in the Italian valleys, as well as chamois. The latter, though fewer on the French side, still form interesting herds. A reserve has been created in the valleys of La Diosaz and Bérard and the Aiguilles Rouges massif. Wood grouse, rock partridges, hazelhen and ptarmigan are the predominant birds, under the sharp eye of the many golden eagles. In the Swiss Val Ferret and the area round Trient are beautiful reserves of deer and roebuck, hunting of which is strictly limited.

All in all the valley of Chamonix is the supreme example of a new mountain civilisation born of tourism.

Since 1965, when the road tunnel under Mont-Blanc was opened, the valley has enjoyed a new source of profit as one of the most frequented routes between Northern Europe and Italy.

A narrow gauge electric railway with a central rail connects Le Fayet to Martigny, in the Rhône valley, running through Chamonix, Argentière, Vallorcine and the granite terraces of Finhaut and Salvan. It passes under the Col des Montets through a tunnel in which there is also a path for pedestrians, in winter time the only route linking Vallorcine and Chamonix. But before and above everything else, the Mont-Blanc massif is the kingdom of mountaineers and skiers, and what a kingdom, dominated by Mont-Blanc the majestic!

**ROGER FRISON-ROCHE.**

## Mont-Blanc

Keep a careful eye on Mont-Blanc for signs of the weather ahead:
- if it wears its cap, it promises storms,
- if it rides its donkey, it forecasts clouds and rain
- if it smokes its pipe, strong winds are coming.

The 'cap' is a cloud bank crowning the mountain.

The 'donkey' is a double line of clouds looking like two great ears spreading out to the east: blown by the west wind they condense on the cold summit, to fall as rain further away in warmer air.

The 'smoke' is snow being blown away from the summit.

The village of Les Houches has been chosen as the starting point of the Tour du Mont-Blanc because it is close to the SNCF railway station on the Saint-Gervais-le

Fayet/Chamonix/Martigny line and will shortly be accessible by way of the new 'Route Blanche' motorway. The railway came to Chamonix in 1901 and to Argentière in 1906. These were important technical achievements. Les Houches was also chosen because it is on the section of the GR5, Holland to the Mediterranean, which runs from the Lake of Geneva to Nice or Menton.

The tour can of course be started at any other point accessible by rail or motor road, or from those sections of the GR5 lying immediately to the north or south. Walkers arriving from the north on the GR5, passing through Chablais, Faucigny, Sixt and Col d'Anterne, will join the TMB - Tour of Mont-Blanc - at the Col du Brévent. Those coming from the south through Beaufortin will join it near the Michelin boundary-stone at the 'false' Col de la Croix-du-Bonhomme at 2,483 metres, close to the CAF refuge.

The TMB follows the same route as the GR5 from Les Houches as far as the 'false' Col de la Croix-du-Bonhomme and on to Les Chapieux, and again from the Col du Brévent back to Les Houches.

## LES HOUCHES

On leaving Les Houches SNCF station, go down and cross the River Arve close to the road-bridge along the dam and turn right, on to the tarmac road which climbs up to the village of Les Houches itself.

**Warning** While the new motorway is under construction, the route of the GR5 between the SNCF railway station and Les Houches village is having to be modified from time to time to fit in with work in progress.

Turn right again, through the village, passing in front of the church to reach the terminus of the cable-car to Bellevue. Pass the cable-car station, and after 50 metres turn left and follow the path which goes to the Col de Voza, passing the hotel Schuss Battendier (see map ref 20).

**2:00**

Detour *15 mins*
### LES CHAVANTS

**Detour** At the hotel, turn right on to the tarmac road to the junction by the physics summer school, to reach the Les Chavants refuge, belonging to Les Amis de la Nature, at La Côte near the foot of the Le Prarion cable railway.

The GRs carry on climbing, passing in succession the Chalets de l'APAS, du Nais and de la Frie. Cross a stream and shortly afterwards, leave the road leading straight on up to Le Prarion, and take a footpath to the left, climbing up through hairpin bends. After passing through woods and copses, over rather swampy ground, you come to a grassy plateau dominated by a hotel, and the Col de Voza.

### Le Col de Voza

*1,653m*
*(see map ref 21)*
*Col in the alpine pastures between Le Prarion and the Bellevue plateau; Station on the Tramway du Mont-Blanc from Saint-Gervais-le-Fayet to the Nid d'Aigle; this rack-railway, built between 1902 and 1904 easily climbs the 25 degree slope from Saint-Gervais in about 50 minutes.*

From the Col de Voza, the GR5 and GRTMB descend the south-facing slope along a beautiful wide track, pass in front of the Chalet du Fioux at 1,520 metres and reach the edge of the hamlet of Le Crozat. There you join a small road to the old village of Bionnassay.

**0:20**

**Detour** *1hr*
## LE PRARION
⌂ ✕

*1,967m*
*Hôtel du Prarion; Accessible*
*from Les Houches by chair-*
*lift and by a dry footpath, or*
*from the Col de Voza by the*
*GR path l'Avant-Pays du*
*Mont-Blanc; Waymarking of*
*this local GR in progress.*

**Detour** Turn right at the Col to reach the hotel, then carry on walking to the summit; with beautiful views of Les Aiguilles de Chamonix, the Arve valley, the Rochers des Fiz and the beginning of the Aiguilles de Varan; and to the south the valley of Les Contamines-Montjoie.

**Alternative route** to Les Contamines via the Col de Tricot. From the Col de Voza, take the path heading eastwards across the meadows, more or less following the Tramway du Mont-Blanc line, then gently climb up to Bellevue.

0:25

## Bellevue
*1,781m*
*Intermediate rack-railway*
*station and upper terminus*
*of chair-lift from Les*
*Houches.*

The GR runs south of the railway line and heads east on a good track along the mountain flank to the Chalets de l'Arc.

0:25

## Chalets de l'Arc
*1,794m*

From this point, the path rises slightly in a moraine area, crossing, at 1850 metres, the upper neck of the Glacier de Bionnassay. The Col de Tricot stands out directly ahead, with a few ruins at its base, as a landmark. The crossing directly west is easy and without danger, being flat and stony. Cross a stream over a bridge if the bridge is in place.

**Warning** Beware of the stream after a storm or in springtime. In the spring it is absolutely necessary to avoid this area, because of the high risk of avalanches.

1:10

The GR passes the ruined Chalets de Tricot and follows a number of hairpin bends up a broad combe, to reach the Col de Tricot.

## Col de Tricot
*2,120m*
*Outstanding views of the*
*north face of the Dômes de*
*Miage. The pass lies*
*between the lower peak of*
*Mont Vorassay to the*

The GR descends very steeply in a south-easterly direction, and by a whole series of hairpin bends arrives at the Chalets de Miage.

1:20

**Trees at every level**

Mountain paths change their appearance with the seasons; you may discover them winding among flowers, or covered with fresh snow on yellowing grass, but whatever the season they will guide you among the same trees.

Forests stretch in succession along the slopes, each with its particular procession of shrubs, small plants and animals, offering different varieties at each level, from the valley plains to the summits. Oaks, easy to recognise with their acorns and lobed leaves, make up a large part of the lower forests and flourish at altitudes up to 1,000 metres in the mountains, at which level they often mingle with beeches.

Beautiful trees up to 40 metres tall, beeches, like oaks, flourish in the lower lying northern half of France, but only appear above 800 metres in the Mediterranean mountains. Leaving the oak forests behind, the beech forest makes its own way on up into the mountains, reaching an altitude of about 1,300 metres.

This is where the true mountain stage begins, usually characterised by silver fir trees, recognisable by their short flat needles, often with two white lines underneath and growing separately along each sprig. At a slightly higher altitude the firs give way to another large conifer species, the spruce, whose branches carry long hanging cones and stiff, sharp-pointed needles growing around the sprigs.

Further up the undergrowth becomes more bushy, trees more spaced out, and they seem less dark and dense. No silver firs any more. Here you will find the mountain or pitch pine growing at an altitude of 1,500 metres or more, marking a further step into the high universe of the Alps.

Finally, the Arolla, or Swiss stone pine, the only conifer here with needles grouped in fives and an edible seed, holds the altitude record at 2,500 metres. It is found only in the Alps.

The stone pine grows mainly among low bushes, among which are junipers, rather prickly, with short needles grouped in threes. At around 2,000 metres, a scrub area, the sub-alpine level, marks the transition into the high alpine level consisting largely of the grassy pasture lands known as alpages.

Around 3,000 metres, the vegetation consists only of a few mosses and lichens: above this a climate prevails which is often compared to that of polar regions.

*(Quoted from Dans la Montagne, Editions Hatier)*

*northwest easily accessible within 20 minutes and the Pointe Inférieure de Tricot to the south east.*

### CHALETS DE MIAGE

*1,559m*

0:35

### CHALETS DU TRUC

*1,720m*
*The Truc plateau, with the grassy summit of Mont Truc to the north, offers a panoramic view of the Glacier de Miage, the Col de Miage, and the 5 Dômes de Miage.*

1:05

### Junction

0:10

### La Frasse

*1,263m*

0:10

### LES CONTAMINES-MONTJOIE

*1,164m*
*Interesting retable and side panels in 18th century church; 17th century statue*

**Junction** The local GR Tour du Pays du Mont-Blanc, coming from Le Champel on the GR5 to the north west, joins the GRTMB Alternative. The GRTMB Alternative and the local GR share the same route south west towards Les Contamines-Montjoie as far as the path to the Chalets d'Armancette, just before La Frasse.

After crossing two bridges over the Miage stream, the path climbs up westwards to a depression from which it reaches the Chalets du Truc.

The GR heads south west on an old mule track now open to 4 wheel drive cars, running down into meadowland, then a forest, ignoring on the right a path leading to La Gruvaz. After a long stretch of undergrowth, the path passes close to a TCF viewpoint at 1,512 metres, continues down to the bottom of a small valley, and then a wide combe, rapidly losing height. You pass two barns and, farther down on the left, the path going off to Armancette, and a few steps later you reach a junction.

The local GR Tour du Pays de Mont-Blanc leaves the GRTMB Alternative Route.

The local GRTMB follows the path, left, to the Chalets d'Armancette and on to rejoin the GR5 at Nant Borrant. The GRTMB Alternative continues westwards down to the hamlet of La Frasse.

Cut across hairpin bends in the road going down between farms and chalets, to reach the church of Les Contamines-Montjoie.

To rejoin the regular GRTMB take the road in a westerly direction, turn left on to the D902 running south, and take the first turning to the right westwards, in order to reach the hamlet of La Vy, just upstream of Nivorin.

**0:15**

*of Saint-François de Sales;
Dedication Festival 15
August; Strategically
important since the Gallo-
Roman epoch as an access
point for the Cols du
Bonhomme and du Joly,
leading to the Tarentaise
and Beaufortin respectively.
In the middle ages the
Lords of Faucigny built
Montjoie castle, but after
1355 when the Counts of
Savoy took control it lost its
importance and fell into ruin.
By 1500 both castle and
village were completely
abandoned. Between 1700
and 1750 a new village was
built, and a new parish
founded in 1758, which has
become a mountaineering
and ski resort of great
renown.*

### LA VY OR LA VIE
⌂ ✕

*(see map ref 23)*

**Junction** The TMB Alternative via the Col de
Tricot rejoins the regular TMB and GR5.

0:55

**BIONNASSAY**

*1,314m*
*Typical mountain hamlet of the Saint-Gervais commune; the starting point of early attempts to conquer Mont-Blanc.*

The GR continues along the path which runs past a former chapel, then winds through a wood, and comes down to the bank of the Bionnassay stream which it crosses by a newly built bridge. Then bear right and carry on to the hamlet of Le Champel.

0:50

**Le Champel**
*1,201m*
*(see map ref 22)*
*A crossways with the local GR Tour du Pays de Mont-Blanc, which runs north west to the Col de la Forclaz and Les Houches and south east to the chalets de Miage and then the GR5 at Le Nant-Borrant. Plans for modifying the route of the GR5 and GRTMB are currently being studied by the tourist services of Les Contamines-Montjoie, with a view to finding a pleasanter path along the level.*

The GRTMB and GR5 cross the D902 road from Bionnay and Saint-Gervais.

Shortly after the chapel at Le Champel, near to an old fountain, turn sharp left and go down a gravel road; when this turns right, carry straight on along the old track, through some bushes to the first chalets of the hamlet of La Villette. At the end of the hamlet near a beautiful fountain with two pools, the GRs swing left along the hill-side. After the hamlet of Quart, you reach a small road. Do not take this road, but turn immediately left up the school path towards La Gruvaz. Follow a made-up path to the Miage stream and the refreshment-bar of the Gorges de la Gruvaz. In front of the chalet take the path running above the left bank of the stream with yellow and blue local waymarking, to Tresse-d'en-Haut; then by a tarmac road to Tresse.

**Detour** *40 mins*
**LES BERNARDS**

*850m*
*Take the small road which descends to Bionnay.*

1:00

**TRESSE**

*1,020m*
*Hamlet on the outskirts of Les Contamines-Montjoie; SAT bus stop for Les Contamines and Saint-Gervais.*

Cross the D902 and go down by a small road to cross the Bon Nant stream and reach the hamlet of Le Quy. With beautiful views of the Dômes de Miage and Aiguille de la Bérangère, the GRs, on a tarmac road, but with little traffic, pass successively through the villages of Les Hoches, Le Molliet, La Revenaz and Le Cugnonnet to reach Nivorin.

**NIVORIN**

*1,161m*
*Hamlet on the outskirts of Les Contamines-Montjoie.*

From Nivorin, along a wide path across meadows, the GRs proceed to the hamlet of La Vy or La Vie and the CAF Chalet Bellevue.

## Les Contamines

The nature reserve of Les Contamines covers about 5,500 hectares, with its lowest point at about 1,170 metres near Cugnon, and its highest the summit of the Aiguille de Tré-la-Tête at 3,892 metres. It runs along the right bank of the Bon Nant from Champelet in the north to the Dômes de Miage. On the east and south its boundary follows the line of the high peaks of Tré-la-Tête, l'Aiguille des Glaciers, Mont Tondu, the Tête Nord des Fonds, the Col des Fours and Col de la Croix-du-Bonhomme; its western limits are the Aiguilles de la Pennaz, de la Gicle, and de Roselette.

**Detour** *15 mins*
**LES CONTAMINES-MONTJOIE**

0:10

*1,164m*
*Turn left off the D902, cross the Bon Nant stream, and take the road left into the village.*

**LA VY OR LA VIE**

0:10

*(see map ref 23)*

**Junction** The GRTMB Alternative route from the Col de Voza rejoins the GR5 and regular GRTMB. The GRs carry on to Le Lay.

**LE LAY**

*1,170m*

0:30

The GRs join the D902 and turn left, crossing a stream, then turn right along a gravel track going upstream on the right bank. Pass some chalets, the climbing school and cross the stream again to reach the chapel of Notre-Dame-de-la-Gorge.

**NOTRE-DAME-DE-LA-GORGE**

*(see map ref 24)*
*1,210m*
*Much frequented pilgrimage site at the foot of the Gorge de Bon Nant and end of the D902 road; Sanctuary with curious polychromatic statues, former hermitage of Saint-Antoine; outdoor Stations of the Cross.*

0:45

From the Notre-Dame-de-la-Gorge chapel, the GRs continue up the right bank of the Bon Nant, along the paved path, formerly a Roman road, known as Rochassets. In some places cut through the rock, they climb steeply up, hemmed in between the walls of the narrow gorge and the stream. The route here runs through the Nature Reserve of Les Contamines-Montjoie, one of the seven reserves established in Haute-Savoie. Cross the Bon Nant by the Roman bridge of la Téna at 1,392 metres shortly after its confluence with the Tré-la-Tête stream, and take a path passing among some barns, which leads to the Chalet-Hotel du Nant-Borrant.

## CHALET-HOTEL DU NANT-BORRANT

⌂ ⚿ ✗ ⚏

*(see map ref 25)*
*1,460m*
*Beautifully situated at the top of a clearing dominated on the east by the Dômes de Miage, the Tré-la-Tête glacier and Mont Tondu.*

0:45

## LA BALME

⌂ ⚏

*1,706m*
*(see map ref 26)*

0:20

## Sluice on the Bon-Nant

*1,900m*

**Detour** *1 hr*
## LES LACS JOVET

⚿

*2,175m and 2,194m*
*Trout fishing licence required*

**Junction** The local GR Tour du Pays du Mont-Blanc from Le Champel via the Chalets de Miage joins the GR5 and GRTMB, and shares the same route as far as La Balme.

The GRs go past the chalet, across the Lancher stream and into the Bois de La Role, a very beautiful wood of conifers.

**Warning** Be careful not to mistake the rather similar forestry service marks for the GR waymarking: a red line of variable width on white background.

Leaving the wood, continue straight along the wide path, crossing a broad level alpine pasture and passing just below on your left the chalets of La Giette, then those of La Role. After a fountain on the left of the path climb up to La Balme.

**Junction** The local GR Tour de Beaufortin joins the GR5 and GRTMB and shares the GR5 route as far as the Plan de la Lai; the local GR Tour du Pays du Mont-Blanc leaves the GR5 and runs west towards the Col de la Fenêtre and Praz-sur-Arly. It shares the same route as the local GR Tour du Beaufortin as far as the Col de Véry. The GR5 and GRTMB continue southwards together.

From the Chalet, the GRs lead south on a very poor track up a steep cliff crossed by the Bon Nant stream. Before long, you come to a sluice on the Bon-Nant.

**Warning** In bad weather, it is better to use instead the good EDF track to the right, going round to the west, and meeting the GRs again at Plan Jovet.

**Detour** Leave the GRs close to the sluice gate on the Bon Nant and after crossing the stream, take the track going north east which runs up to the beautiful Lacs Jovet, situated below Mont Jovet and Mont Tondu.

The GRs cross the Plan Jovet in a south-easterly

2:15

## Plan des Dames

*A small flat area, with a vast burial mound, which according to legend covers the mortal remains of an English lady and her maid-servant, killed during a terrible storm. Traditionally, to commemorate the tragedy and avoid bad luck, every passing traveller adds a stone to the mound.*

## Le Col du Bonhomme

*2,329m*

*Dominated on the left, east, by a two-headed rock, traditionally called Le Rocher du Bonhomme et de la Bonne Femme; designated site. Views north to the long line of Val Montjoie, north east to the Tré-la-Tête massif, south and south west down to the valley of Les Chapieux and the mountains of Beaufortin; south east to the Tarentaise and Mont Pourri.*

0:50

## Col de la Croix-du-Bonhomme

*2,483m*

*Not in fact the true Col de la Croix-du-Bonhomme, which is 500 metres to the south beyond the CAF refuge, as IGN maps show, but a Michelin distance marker erected here before the 1939-1945 war showed this as the Col, and the mistake has continued.*

0:10

direction. When the gradient increases, the path takes a south-westerly direction, and climbs another steep section leading to the Plan des Dames.

After a steep curve over screes, where substantial névés remain late in the season, we reach the Col du Bonhomme.

The GRs bear south south east, taking a path to the left which climbs up - not the one going down. After a short rise over stony ground, walking becomes easier; this traversée or crossing remains snow covered until late in the season, and, after crossing the Nant des Lotharets stream, leads without much change of altitude, to the Col de la Croix-du-Bonhomme.

**Junction** The GRTMB Alternative route to La Ville des Glaciers via the Col des Fours leaves the GR5 and GRTMB. This is a much more beautiful and mountainous route than the regular GRTMB.

**Warning** Late snow conditions on the Col des Fours and the difficulty of finding a path between the Plan des Fours and Chalets des Tufs mean this Alternative should only be attempted in good weather conditions and by experienced walkers.

The GR5 and GRTMB head south from the Michelin marker at the false Col de la Croix-

## REFUGE CAF DE LA CROIX-DU-BONHOMME
⌂ ✕

*2,443m*
*(see map ref 27)*
*Orientation table. Very*
*beautiful views over Le*
*Beaufortin and La*
*Tarentaise.*

**1:20**

## CHALETS DE LA RAJA
⌂

*1,790m*
*Chalets open in Summer-*
*time, water, milk products.*
**0:30**  *End of the motor road from*
*Les Chapieux.*

## LES CHAPIEUX
ⓗ ⌂ ▲ ✕ ⚖

*1,554m*
*18km by road from Bourg-*
*Saint-Maurice on the N202;*
*No public transport except*
*shuttle bus to the Auberge*
*de la Nova.*

du-Bonhomme, over a small hill where the refuge comes into view and past a hydrant, to arrive at the CAF Refuge de la Croix-du-Bonhomme.

**Junction** The GR Tour du Mont-Blanc leaves the GR5. To complete Walk 1 follow the GRTMB and local GR Tour du Beaufortin Alternative route to Les Chapieux and the D902 motor road.

To follow the GRTMB from the refuge, it is essential to turn left, eastwards under an electric power line. If waymarks are hidden by snow, head for the second EDF pylon.

**Warning** Do not be misled by tracks left in the snow by walkers who have been able to come straight down to Les Chapieux earlier in the season. If in doubt, do not hesitate to ask the refuge keeper.

The GRTMB carries on across alpine pastures up to the Chalets de Plan Varraro, and then continues downwards across pastures, to reach, the Chalets de la Raja.

The GRTMB takes a well marked footpath, following short cuts formerly used by agricultural machinery, down to the village of Les Chapieux.

This is the end of Walk 1. Walk 2 'Tour du Mont-Blanc' continues from here. Les Chapieux is also the starting point for Walk 3.

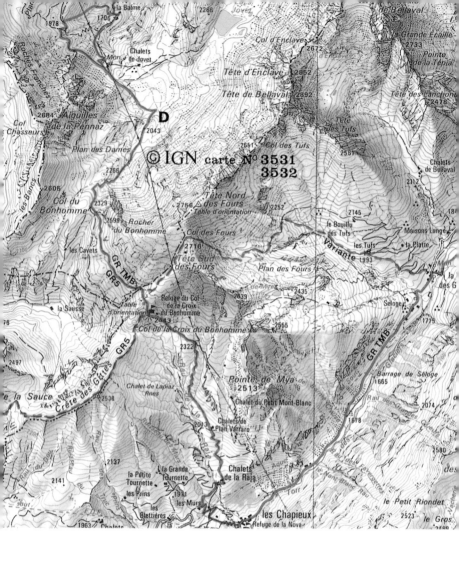

## LES CHAPIEUX

🏠 ⌂ ⛺ 🍴 🚉

*1,554m*

*Unfortunately, the road followed by the TMB from Les Chapieux to the Col de la Seigne is now open for cars as far as the chalets of Lanchettes.*

1:20

In the village of Chapieux take the tarmac road in front of the Hotel du Soleil along the right bank of the Torrent des Glaciers, past a series of small dams. The road climbs gently through rather bare countryside and reaches Séloge.

**SÉLOGE**
⌂ ✗ ⚖
*1,809m*
*Possibility of overnight shelter in barns.*

0:10

**La Ville-des-Glaciers**
*1,789m*
*Group of shepherds' chalets, on right bank of Glaciers stream, facing l'Aiguille des Glaciers.*

**LES CHAPIEUX**

0:40

**Chalets de la Raja**
*1,689m*
*High mountain chalets normally inhabited in summertime; motor road from Les Chapieux ends at this point.*

0:40

**Chalets de Plan Vararo**
*2,013m*

1:25

**REFUGE DU COL DE LA CROIX-DU-BONHOMME**
⌂ ✗
*2,443m*
*There is an orientation table; views over Le Beaufortain and La Tarentaise.*

0:10

**Col de la Croix-du-Bonhomme**
*2,483m*
*This is not in fact the true Croix du Bonhomme pass, which lies beyond the refuge to the south, at 2,412m, as shown on IGN maps; before the 1939-1945 war a Michelin waymarker was sited here, claiming this to be the pass, and the error has stuck.*

0:40

Continue along the same road; the valley widens and here the high Vallée des Glaciers and the Aiguille des Glaciers peak come into view. Cross the Tufs stream coming down from the Plan des Fours, to reach La Ville-des-Glaciers.

**Junction** The TMB Alternative route from Col des Fours rejoins the GRTMB.

**Alternative route** The GRTMB follows a well marked country road, made up from old shortcuts, to the Chalets de la Raja.

The GR follows a path up into the mountain pastures to the Chalets de Plan Vararo.

The path continues to climb, first through pastureland and then over rocky slopes, passing close to a ruined military shelter, to reach the Refuge of the Col de la Croix-du-Bonhomme.

The path climbs for a short distance to the Col de la Croix-du-Bonhomme.

**Junction** The GRTMB joins the GR5 from the Chamoix valley to the north, and the TMB alternative route from La Ville des Glaciers via the Col des Fours.

From the Michelin marker the TMB Alternative route takes the track right, to the north east, which is often covered in snow even in August. Pass close to a ruined house, then under an electric power line, and across easy rocks or snow patches, to reach the Col des Fours.

### Le Col des Fours
*2,265m*
**Detour** *1hr*
### Tête Nord des Fours
*2,756m*
*Famous climber H.B. de Saussure and guide Pierre Balmat on 7 August 1781 first found and praised this vast panoramic view, one of the most beautiful in this part of the Mont Blanc range.*

1:20

### Chalets des Tufs
*1,993m*

0:20

### La Ville-des-Glaciers
*(Map ref E)*

0:15

**Detour** From the col, follow the ridge running north, along an easy path to the top, where there is an orientation table.

From the col the TMB Alternative turns down to the right along the north east side of the Tête Sud des Fours below some rock terraces where there may be late névé, but keep away from the base of the cliff in case of rock falls. On reaching the level Plan des Fours, the GR follows the right bank of a stream, going northwards. The path becomes steeper, and reaches a second level area and crosses this in a north-easterly direction. Just before reaching a larger stream which comes down from the Tête Nord du Fours, turn right and head south east.

**Warning** The next part of the route, across a steep and swampy alpine pasture requires great care.

The path goes down a badly marked stony slope; crosses the stream, and continues, still in a south-easterly direction, along the side of the mountain, gradually moving away from the stream. Here there is no proper path, only cattle and sheep tracks, till you arrive at the Chalets des Tufs.

The GR avoids a private path, and skirts in front of the farmhouse on a well marked track going southwards.

**Warning** The farmer who owns these pastures requests walkers not to take short cuts across the meadows, so as to avoid frightening the livestock.

This leads directly to the hamlet of La Ville des Glaciers, where, after about 20 minutes walking time, you rejoin the regular TMB.

The GR passes below the chalets and across the Glaciers stream, turns immediately left and climbs gradually beside the stream. Cross the stream - this may be difficult early in the year - which comes down from the Montagne de la Seigne, to reach the Chalets des Mottets.

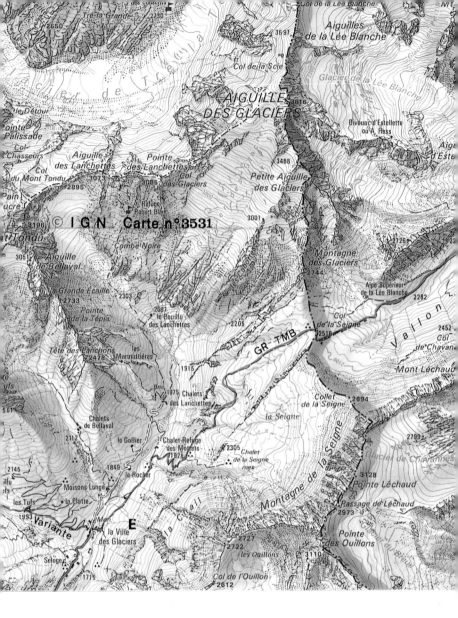

## CHALETS DES MOTTETS

⌂ ✕ ☖

1,978m

2:35

The path curves above the chalets and climbs through a series of hairpin bends over a spur. Go on past a ruin, and then past a path leading off on the right to the chalet de la Seigne. The slope is gentle and after a long but quite easy ascent you reach the Col de la Seigne - or, on some maps, 'de Séjane'.

## Col de la Seigne

There is some evidence that this pass was already used in ancient times. A Roman road 'Cremonis jugum' gave direct access to the town of Vienne in Isère; wonderful views of the Italian side of Mont-Blanc with the high ridges of Brouillard and Peuterey, and the elegant Aiguilles des Dames Anglaises. The Col de la Seigne is a gateway to the Val d'Aosta, a valley criss-crossed by streams running into the River Doire, and dominated by the most impressive summits of the Alps : Mont-Blanc, Grand-Paradis, Grand-Combin, Cervin, Mont-Rose. The valley enjoys a certain regional autonomy, and French is spoken fluently by its very welcoming population.

### Col de la Seigne

*2,516m*
*Marked by a big cairn on the frontier between France and Italy. Situated between l'Aiguille des Glaciers (3,816m) and the Montagne de la Seigne, on the watershed between the Mediterranean and Adriatic formed by the alpine range separating the Val d'Aosta in Italy from the Tarentaise.*

0:50

From the Col de la Seigne, when there is still snow, go down through the combe on the left to the north east; otherwise go down on the Italian side, taking the middle path going eastwards, and ignoring a track on the right which bends south towards the Col de Chavannes - 2,550 metres.

**Warning** Look out for névés on this descent.

Cross a few gullies and then a fast flowing stream at the base of a rock. Next take a track bending towards the ruins of an old 'Carabiniers' - police - post and then leading to the top chalet of La Lée Blanche at 2,282 metres. From there it descends and then levels out to reach the chalets of l'Alpe inférieure de la Lée Blanche.

### Alta Via Tours

The path to the Col de Chavannes is part of the Italian 'Alta Via' or 'High Altitude' Tour No 2, which shares the same route as the TMB up to the Col de Chécroui and on to Courmayeur by the TMB Alternative through Dolonne. The 'Alte Vie' Tours 1 and 2 of the Val d'Aosta are two beautiful footpaths - about 282 kilometres long, created in 1980 by the Val d'Aosta Tourist Services. Route No 1 runs from Gressoney to Courmayeur by way of Breuil-Cervinia, the Valpelline and Saint-Rémy, through some quite high cols such as the Col Supérieur des Cimes Blanches - 2,982 metres and Fort Bivacco Rivolta - 2,906 metres. No 2 starts from Château-Champorcher and crosses the Grand Paradis massif from west to east up to Courmayeur, also through high altitude cols: Lauson at 3,296 metres, l'Entrelor at 3,002 metres.

These important routes are marked by yellow triangles and arrows. The Office du Tourisme at Courmayeur has a leaflet about them.

© IGN carte N° 3631

## L'Alpe inférieure de la Lée Blanche
*2,035m*
*Shepherds' chalets and barracks in poor condition.*
**Detour** *10 mins*
### REFUGE ELISABETTA SOLDINI
⌂ ✗

0:45

## LAC DE COMBAL BARRAGE
🍸 🚌
*2,020m*
*Retaining dyke with sluice regulating flow of water from the lake. On the left bank of the Doire, a path goes up to the Lac du Miage.*

1:00

## LAC DE COMBAL BARRAGE

0:45

## CANTINE DE LA VISAILLE
✗ 🚌
*1,659m*

0:50

**Detour** The CIA refuge is situated just above the chalets. From the refuge you can return to the chalets by the gravel road, or one of the many short cuts that go down to the flat plain of the Lac de Combal. Follow the road, going north west and then north east - it is unfortunately open to cars - across the wide marsh, known as the 'Lac' de Combal, with its varied alpine flora. Here the valley narrows, blocked downstream by a colossal moraine created by the Glacier du Miage. A footpath leads up on to the moraine if you wish to admire the reflection of the mountains in the lake.

The GR now reaches the Lac de Combal barrage.

**Junction** The TMB Alternative route via Val Veni leaves the GRTMB.
From here walkers have a choice of three routes to Courmayeur.
1. The TMB Alternative route through the Val Veni: about 2 hrs walking time. Un-waymarked till after the Plan Pouquet, as it follows the road. Not a pleasant route because of traffic, but useful in bad weather or for walkers in a hurry. In this valley 6 camp sites are open to walkers.
2. The regular TMB route via Col Chécroui: about 4 hrs 30 mins.
3. The regular TMB as far as Col Chécroui, then taking the shorter Alternative route through Dolonne, in all, about 3 hrs 45 mins.

**Alternative route** to Notre-Dame-de-Guérison via Val Veni. Just before the barrage, the regular TMB bears off to the right. Ignore this, and instead continue on the road, which runs along the left bank of the River Doire de Veni through a narrow gorge for 3 kilometres, then crosses to the right bank to the chalets of Cantine de la Visaille.

A short cut off the road brings you to the chalets de Miage at 1,569 metres at the junction with a road leading across the wide Veni plain which is crowded in summer and at weekends - and up to l'Aiguille Noire with its bar and restaurant. From this beautiful grassy plateau, surrounded by fir-trees, there are marvellous views of the Mont-Blanc chain. At the north east end of the

Plan Veni, you come to the Chalets Purtud.

**CHALETS PURTUD**
(H) 🚌
*1,489m*
*Situated on the far left bank
of the Doire.*

0:20

**Junction** A little farther along the road, the Alternative route rejoins the regular GRTMB from Col Chécroui, which arrives at the chapel of Notre-Dame-de-la-Guérison.

**La Chapelle de Notre-
Dame-de-la-Guérison**
*1,440m*

**Chalet de l'Alpe
supérieure de l'Arp
Vieille**
*2,303m*
*Panoramic views of the
Italian side of Mont-Blanc
massif, with, from left to
right, the glaciers du Miage,
du Brouillard and de
Freiney, starting points of
the most difficult climbs of
the massif.*

1:20

Circle around the Chalet de l'Arp Vieille and continue climbing. At about 1,453 metres the TMB crosses the northern crest of Mont Favre, then descends to a wide basin watered by a stream coming down from the Col de Youla. Ignore on your right a path bearing east up to Col de Youla, and continue in a north-easterly direction, passing close to a small lake and following a path along a ledge running down to Lac Chécroui.

**Lac Chécroui**
*2,165m*
*Pretty lake, reflecting Mont-
Blanc. From here you can
reach the upper terminus of
the chair-lift going down to
the Plan Chécroui, where
the cable-car leaves for
Courmayeur.*

0:20

The footpath continues along the ledge and down to Col Chécroui.

**COL CHÉCROUI**
△ ✕
*1,956m*

1:45

**Alternative route** to Courmayeur through Dolonne. From Col Chécroui take the path to the right marked with red crosses, heading eastwards, passing in succession the chalets of Pra-Neiron, Plan Chécroui - where a dormitory site is open June to September and La Goletta, to arrive at Dolonne.

**DOLONNE**
(H) ✕

Carry on down, crossing the Doire and the main road, to Courmayeur.

**COURMAYEUR**
(H) ✕ 🍷 ⚒ 🚌 🛈
*1,224m*

## COL CHÉCROUI

**1:30**

Due to the construction of a ski-lift and the opening of an international ski-run, the lie of the land around the Col Chécroui has been disturbed. Go down to the left, first in a north-westerly direction, then north east. The GR passes under the cables of a chair-lift, follows the new ski-run, then becomes a path again. Further down, just before the path leading to the Chalets Peindein you reach La Fodze.

Leave the Chalets Peindein on the right at 1,703 metres. A little further on, the GR joins the Val Veni road, not far from the hotel-restaurant of Plan Pouquet at 1,500 metres, and continues along it to the chapel of Notre-Dame-de-la-Guérison.

## La Chappelle de Notre-Dame-de-la-Guérison

*To the west of Entrèves, on the other side of the valley, the entrance of the Mont-Blanc tunnel can be seen in the distance. Linking France to Italy, and Chamonix to Courmayeur, this road tunnel is very important from both economic and touristic points of view. Built between April 1963 and July 1965 and 11.6 kilometres long, its overall width is 8.6 metres and it supports some 2,480 vertical metres of rock under l'Aiguille du Midi.*

**1:00**

**Junction** The Alternative route via Val Veni, rejoins the regular GRTMB.

The road bends around with the Italian Val Ferret spreading away on the left and Entrèves and the confluence of the two Doires just below.

The road continues to descend and crosses the Doire - or Dora Baltea as it is called in Italy, which joins the River Po a few kilometres north east of Turin - either by La Saxe. or La Villette, to reach the tourist resort of Courmayeur.

## COURMAYEUR
🏠 ✗ ☕ �- ━ 🛈

*1,224m*

*Very old town at what has been a busy crossways since early times. Greek historian Polybius mentioned, among transalpine passes used in*

**Junction** The Alternative route via Italian Val Ferret leaves the GRTMB.

From Courmayeur, walkers have a choice of several local excursions and ways of reaching Lavachey in the Italian Val Ferret.

**0:30**

*the mid 2nd century BC, the road 'through the country of the Salassi': Courmayeur was then the important Roman town, Curia Major, close to the Alpis Graia road leading to the Col du Petit-Saint-Bernard, and on the road leading into Gaul by the 'Cremonis jugum', or Col de la Seigne.*

1. The regular GRTMB which ascends the Val Sapin and reaches Lavachey by the Col Sapin and the Pas-entre-deux-Sauts: a long established route avoiding motor traffic.

2. The un-waymarked Alternative route by way of the Italian Val Ferret on a narrow tarmac road, which can be very busy. Useful in bad weather, or for walkers in a hurry.

3. Take the bus from Courmayeur to Lavachey.

4. Stroll for one or two days on local waymarked paths returning to Courmayeur or La Palud to sleep, before continuing on the TMB.

5. Make an excursion to the Col du Géant, or even l'Aiguille du Midi and Chamonix and back: see the Alternative route below.

**COURMAYEUR**

**Alternative route** to Lavachey via the Italian Val Ferret. Un-waymarked, as it follows the road. The stage to Lavachey - and on to Arnuva - can also be covered by bus. From Courmayeur, take the road running northwards above the hamlet of la Saxe; it crosses over and then under the main road and then the Val de Ferret branch of the Doire by the Les Chèvres bridge, and after passing Entrèves on the left, arrives at La Palud.

**1:00**

**Detour** *5 mins*
**ENTRÈVES**
🏠 🚡
*1,306m*
*Large village with 14th century castle. Shortly after the bridge and before reaching La Palud, turn left into the village.*

**LA PALUD**
🏠 ⛺ 🔱 🍴 🚡 🚌
*1,360m*
**Detour**
**Le Col du Géant**
*3,322m*

**Detour** Take the the cable-car from La Palud in two stages, first to the Refuge Torino at 3,332 metres, and then to the Pointe Helbronner at 3,462 metres on the French-Italian frontier. Those who wish can extend this excursion by taking a cable-car to l'Aiguille du Midi at 3,842 metres, and from there, the cable-car which goes down to Chamonix.

**1:45**

From La Palud head north east across woods and meadows, still keeping to the road, to Planpincieux.

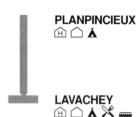

**PLANPINCIEUX**

Continue on the road up the right bank of the Doire, passing on the right the hamlet of Neyron and on the left, those of Le Pont, Tronchey and Pra Sec. Soon after, the road forks right across the stream to the town of Lavachey.

**LAVACHEY**

*1,642m*

**Junction** The Alternative route via Italian Val Ferret rejoins the regular GRTMB.

The GRTMB takes a minor road leading towards Val Sapin, reaching first the hamlets of Villair.

**Villair**
*1,327m*

Go through the hamlets and continue climbing on a good path. At the edge of the forest, the GR follows the left bank of a stream, then crosses it at 1,409 metres. Ignore a path on the left, and also a 2nd which leads to the Mont de la Saxe.

**Detour** *3hrs 30 mins*
**Col Sapin via Mont de la Saxe**

**Detour** Take the 2nd path left, climbing up past the Chalets du Pré.

**CHALETS DU PRÉ**

From the Chalets it is possible to go down to Planpincieux within 1 hour 30 minutes by a path forking left with local waymarks crossed in red. To reach Col Sapin continue along Mont de la Saxe up to the south base of Tête Bernada; bear right through a pass between a summit and Tête de la Tronche, then on down to Col Sapin.

2:00

The GRTMB continues in a north-easterly direction passing in front of the chalets at la Trappe, then climbing along the right bank of the stream, where local waymarks are red crosses or orange triangles, to reach Chapy. The GR turns sharp right across the stream and up a steep path through a forest of fir and larch, turning right onto a slope called Pra Conduit with a panorama. Ignore the path on the right from Courmayeur via La Suche, and the houses of Curru on the left.

**Curru**
*1,964m*
*At the foot of the Liconi*
*Combe, there is a water*
*point.*

1:30

The GR climbs on across the mountain side, winding and crossing fallen rocks, crosses the stream again, and after several small bends reaches Col Sapin.

**Col Sapin**
*2,436m*
*Between Tête du Curru and*
*Tête de la Tronche.*

1:00

**Pas-entre-deux-Sauts**
*2,542m*

2:30

**Junction**

From the Col Sapin, the GR goes on down the combe, across the Armina stream to reach the Chalets de Séchéron. Take the right-hand path, eastwards behind the chalets, then turn left and climb up to Pas-entre-deux-Sauts.

The path descends steeply, joins the left bank of the Malatra stream and continues along the bottom of the valley to the Chalets de l'Alpe Supérieure de Malatra. It then carries on down through Malatra, with panoramic views of the Mont-Blanc range, and reaches the road up the Italian Val Ferret at a bend just above the town of Lavachey.

**Junction** The GR joins the TMB Alternative route from Courmayeur via the Val Ferret.

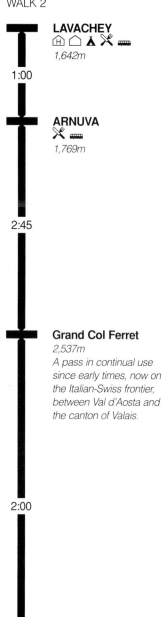

**LAVACHEY**
1,642m

1:00

**ARNUVA**
1,769m

2:45

**Grand Col Ferret**
2,537m
*A pass in continual use
since early times, now on
the Italian-Swiss frontier,
between Val d'Aosta and
the canton of Valais.*

2:00

The GR turns to follow the valley road running up beside the Doire de Ferret, with beautiful views of both Grandes and Petites Jorasses and l'Aiguille de Leschaux, high above the Glacier de Frébouze. After passing a police post it reaches Arnuva.

Continue up the Italian Val Ferret, crossing the stream. The tarmac road gives way to gravel, and at the first bend the GR cuts across the road, climbs up to the right along a winding footpath with a view of the Glacier du Triolet, crosses over a shoulder and passes the ruins of the Refuge Elena. Continue climbing to the Chalets de Pré de Bar.

After passing the Chalets de Pré de Bar at the foot of the Pré de Bar glacier which comes down from Mont-Dolent on the left, the TMB curves round and rises, eastwards at first, reaching some chalets , and then bends north up to the Grand Col Ferret.

**Important** From here on, waymarking will be the Swiss white-red-white lines for mountain paths, and yellow diamond shapes or arrows at lower levels. Walkers may note that efforts have been made to maintain the waymarking at high altitudes by setting the signs on posts along the path, enabling use of the route even in bad snow conditions.

**Warning** Unauthorized camping is forbidden throughout the Swiss Val de Ferret.

The TMB descends gently, bearing left and curving round the top of the wide combe of Revers de la Peula. On reaching the flank, continue along a well marked path, ignoring a small track to the left after about 30 minutes, and cross the alpine meadows of La Chaudière, which offers a rich and varied flora and fauna for those who know how to look for them. The path then runs above a series of gullies.

**Warning** At this point great caution is required.

A steeper slope leads down to the Chalet de la Peula, and from there a broad jeep-track descends rapidly through a series of hairpin bends to the Drance de Ferret stream, crossing it by a small wooden bridge. After a short rise, it joins the road and track coming down from the Grand Saint-Bernard via the Fenêtre de Ferret, just below the Chalets des Ars-dessous. As you follow the road to the left, notice the spruces and larches of the conifer forest named after the village of Ferret.

**Junction**

**Junction** Just before the Pré de Bar chalets, the very beautiful and unfrequented alternative route via Petit Col Ferret, 2,490 metres, leaves the GRTMB and enables walkers to reach Ferret or La Fouly without meeting much traffic.

**Warning** Only to be taken in good weather and fairly late in the season as snow conditions may persist. In the direction Italy to Switzerland, the path is quite steep in places, and sometimes difficult where it passes over loose rock.

**Alternative route** Before the Pré de Bar Chalets, take a path to the left, northwards, which climbs across the flank of the mountain to the foot of the Tête de Ferret. Ignore the track at the bottom of the valley which leads to the end of the Glacier du Pré de Bar. Crossing alpine pastures and some deep ravines, the footpath climbs up to reach the Petit Col Ferret within 2 hours 30 minutes. Pass the Petit Col Ferret, then carry on down, keeping above the south-east rim of the Combe des Fonds, past Crêtet de la Grouille.

5:00

**Warning** The Combe des Fonds is to be avoided on account of rock falls and broken seracs coming down from the glaciers and moraine of Mont-Dolent.

**Le Petit col Ferret**
*2,490m*

Continue down to the the meadow of La Léchère; a good path leads you to rejoin the GRTMB at the villages of Ferret, within 2 hours 15 minutes or La Fouly, 2 hours 30 minutes from the Petit Col Ferret.

**FERRET**

*1,705m*

**Detour**
**Col du Grand Saint-Bernard**

**Detour** From Ferret, take the road south, and fork left at Les Ars-dessous to cross the alpine meadow of Plan de la Chaux at 2,041 metres, and climb to the Lacs de Fenêtre at 2,456 metres. From this point walkers have a choice of 3 routes to the Grand Saint-Bernard and its hospice.

**Warning** These are very beautiful excursions, but must only be undertaken by experienced walkers in good weather conditions.

1. Via the Lacs de Fenêtre 2,456 metres. Yellow waymarking. On the way back you can take the bus at the Col du Grand Saint-Bernard and go down to Orsières to catch the connection to either Ferret or Champex.

2. Via the Col de Fenêtre de Ferret, 8 hours there and back. 2,698 metres. White-red-white waymarking. Quite an easy route, yet giving the impression of a high altitude walk.

0:30

3. Via the Col de la Fenêtre d'en-Haut, 10 hours there and back. 2,724 metres. For experienced hikers. Waymarked. The route ends at the Hospice du Grand Saint-Bernard. On the way back, you can take the bus at the Col du Grand Saint-Bernard and go down to Orsières to catch the connection to either Ferret or Champex.

**Warning** Unauthorised camping is forbidden throughout the valley.

*The road through the Swiss Val Ferret follows the right bank of the Drance de Ferret, and is as pleasant as the high Italian Val Ferret. Alpine pastures, strawberry*

From the village of Ferret, it is possible to get to La Fouly by the road, but the GRTMB follows an untarred path which leaves the road just south of Ferret, going down across the Drance and running right along the left bank of the stream. Ignore various paths on the left, continue

---

**Val Ferret**

'Here there are no concrete towers, no enclosed deer park. The fauna enjoys its natural habitat. Everything here is completely authentic, in Val Ferret, the valley of the three River Drances hemmed in between two mountain ranges, each completely different from the other. On the left bank is the kingdom of granite, all steep slopes, jagged crests, hanging ice-fields, rushing torrents, waterfalls. On the right bank smoother calcareous slopes, grassy and wooded; the pastures rising very high, with a varied and interesting flora, but smaller mountains.'
*(Quoted from Georges Pillet of Martigny).*

fields, evergreen forests enlivened by beautiful waterfalls, and picturesque flowery villages whose chalets with carved balconies are typical of the area, stretch for about 15 kilometres. This road can be travelled by bus from Martigny-Orsières: if so, get off at Issert, unless discouraged by the steep rise to Champex, in which case stay on the bus to Orsières and catch the connection there.

## LA FOULY
⌂ △ ⛺ ✕ 🚠 🚌 🅱
1,610m

Here it may be of interest to consider the nearby landscape and its underlying geology. In effect the moraine of the Glacier de Saleina forms a great barrier some 50 metres high along the whole length of the valley, laid down there during the millennia when the glacier was retreating. Here and there on the picturesque path running along the wooded ridge of the top, walkers will come on enormous granite boulders, the largest, the 'Pierre au Renard', or 'Fox Rock', being more than 4,500 cubic metres in size. The site is designated and protected.

**1:45**

## BRANCHE D'EN HAUT
⌂
1,381m

along the stream, and turn right to cross it again just under the Clou chalet. Turn left along the road to reach the village of La Fouly.

Just before the southern entrance of the village, turn left and cross the Drance de Ferret into the hamlet of A Neuve. The waymarking here is the Swiss Low-level yellow outlined with black. Take the good path to the right between the houses, crossing the stream also called A Neuve - in this area, streams are known as reuses. The GR runs through a beautiful wood of conifers, and above the hamlet of Amône, crosses the Reuse de l'Aumône, and keeping at a short distance from the Drance de Ferret, continues down through woods and meadows. At the 1,370 metres marker a track leads right, across the Drance to Branche d'en Haut.

After crossing the Reuse de Planereuse, the GR runs along beside the Drance de Ferret, following it as far as the Reuse de Saleina.

Cross the Reuse de Saleina to reach the Chalets de Chanton and the village of Praz-de-Fort.

## PRAZ-DE-FORT
Ⓗ ⌂ 🚉 🚌
*1,151m*

**0:20**

## ISSERT
🍷 🚉 🚌
*1,055m*
*Pleasant place, typical of Valais, with many of its wooden houses, barns and granaries built on piles, topped by large flat stones - called lauze- to keep out the rats and mice.*

**1:30**

## CHAMPEX
Ⓗ ⌂ ⛺ 🍴 🚉 🚌
*1,466m*
*Very popular summer resort, beautiful surroundings of the Lac de Champex, between the mountains of Le Catogne and La Breya. The tour round the lake takes 30 minutes and enables walkers to discover a luxuriant flora. From the terrace of the Alpina restaurant, views of Le Grand Combin, Orsières, the Grand Saint-Bernard valley, Le Val d'Entremont and Le Val Ferret.*

**2:15**

## ARPETTE
Ⓗ 🍴
*1,689m*

## La Barme
*2,140m*

The GR goes into the village, crosses the Drance, and immediately turns left, north, towards the typical hamlet Arlaches. A path along the mountain flank, on the right bank of the stream, leads to Issert.

Some 400 metres below Issert, the GR turns left through meadows and woods, on a path with yellow and black waymarks, climbs up and across the Pré-nondes stream, and goes into the forest, passing some old slate quarries and then the Chalets de l'Affe at 1,324 metres and Niolet at 1,319 metres. After a steep slope, it reaches the Champex to Orsières road, close to the swimming pool of Champex.

From Champex, walkers have a choice of 2 routes to the Col de Balme:
1. The regular GRTMB via Bovine at 1,897 metres is easy, but longer than the Alternative, with beautiful views of the Rhône valley and Martigny.
2. The Alternative route via La Fenêtre d'Arpette at 2,665 metres must only be attempted in good weather and by experienced walkers. Magnificent views of the the Glacier du Trient, giving the impression of a high mountain route.

**Alternative route** via La Fenêtre d'Arpette. Go through Champex to the start of the chair-lift to La Breya, and take either the motor road waymarked white-red-white, or the 'Ruisseau' footpath waymarked with green lines which follows the Arpette stream and its waterfalls, through beautiful open woodland, joining the white-red-white track below the Chalet d'Arpette.

After the chalet, ignore the green waymarked path on the left which goes over the Col de la Breya and down into the the Combe d'Orny. The GR passes another chalet, and, becoming more stony, continues along the Arpette stream and after a rock used by a climbing school, reaches La Barme.

Ignore a red waymarked path going ahead to the Col des Ecandies at 2,796 metres and the glacial plateau of Trient, and instead take the

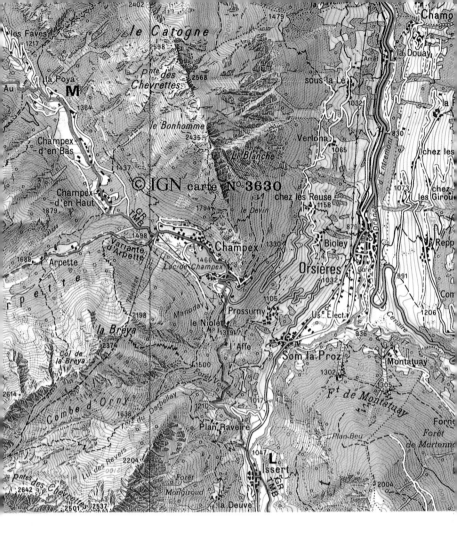

2:50

**La Fenêtre d'Arpette**
*2,671m*
*Narrow pass - hence the
name: Fenêtre = window -
between Le Génépi and the
Pointe des Ecandies -
amidst enormous rocks on*

red-white-red waymarked path to the right,
towards Fenêtre d'Arpette. The slope becomes
steeper and the vegetation thins, then
disappears. Half way up the last very steep
rise you come to a brook flowing under big
rocks, which is the last water point before Prise
du Bisse, and finally reach La Fenêtre d'Arpette.

The GR runs along above the glacier, then
descends on a stony track, losing height very
quickly, and arrives above the Chalet de Vésevy
at 2,096 metres. There you find a path that
continues on a ledge along the tongue of the
glacier, and then enters a forest of magnificent
Swiss stone pines over a century old. After

*the ridge. The view is striking on the Vallon d'Arpette side, looking down on rock falls on all the surrounding summits, but the impression is even greater when, after passing the col, one comes face to face with the majestic and turbulent expanse of the Glacier de Trient immediately below - an unusual sight for a walker.*

**2:15**

several hairpin bends, it reaches the ruins of the Chalet de l'Ourtiers at 1,710 metres, then goes through a larch forest, arriving at La Prise du Bisse.

**Prise du Bisse**
*1,583m*
**Detour** *1 hr*
**COL DE LA FORCLAZ OR PEUTY**
⌂

**Detour** Walkers wishing to stay overnight in this area can take the path along the Bisse to join the regular TMB at Col de la Forclaz in 50 minutes. You can also go down to Le Peuty following the path along the Bisse for 20 minutes then bearing left to reach the hamlet by cutting across the bends on the road to Col de la Forclaz.

**3:35**

The GR crosses the Trient stream then turns left. A little further on, ignore the path on the left going to les Petoudes-d'en-Haut, and climb on up to the sheep pens at Les Grands at 2,113 metres at the foot of the Glaciers des Grands. Shortly afterwards, cross the eastern crest of the Pointe du Midi by a pass cut through the rocks, and pass some sheep pens at Remointse at 2,078 metres. At the 2,055 metres mark you ignore a path to the right which leads down to towards Tsanton des Aroles, and after passing above the Chalet des Herbagères at 2,053 metres, rejoins the regular TMB coming from Col de la Forclaz. After climbing up through a few bends, you reach the Col de Balme.

**COL DE BALME**
⌂ ✕
*2,191m*

**Junction** The Alternative route via La Fenêtre d'Arpette rejoins the GRTMB.

**CHAMPEX**

**1:15**

The GRTMB passes through Champex, continues along the road waymarked with yellow diamonds, turns left on a path going first to Champex-d'en-Haut, then Champex-d'en-Bas. After meeting the road again, take a path to the left and cross the stream, then a small valley, to reach the alpine pasture of Plan de l'Au.

## The Bisses

'Bisse' is a Valaisan word meaning a conduit or irrigation canal, either carved out of rock or made out of wood. With the partial disappearance of mountain agriculture, the bisses have fallen into disuse. But they are true 'historical monuments', and a widespread campaign was undertaken in 1982 to try and save as many of them as possible. At a press conference held by the Association Valaisanne de Tourisme Pédestre on 25 March that year, its President Georges Pillet stated:

'The very unusual and interesting history of our bisses is a striking illustration of the people's fight for water, which was nowhere so hard and desperate as in the central part of Valais. Our bisses - for there are none in the other cantons, are among the earliest works of art that exemplify Switzerland's rural genius. In the later Middle Ages, murderers and other criminals were not hanged, but condemned to go and carve bisses out of sheer rock faces along the mountain sides. If a criminal happened to fall over the edge, that settled the matter. If he survived the work on one bisse, he was sent to work on another. Our ancestors built the bisses without help or subsidy, by the strength of their arms alone, driven by sheer will-power to create something that was essential to their survival.'

From a study made in 1907 by F. Rauchenstein, the government engineer of Valais, it seems there were 207 bisses between Bellwald and Champex, with a total length of 2,000 kilometres, and the length of the whole network was estimated to be 25,000 kilometres, or 5,000 kilometres more than half the circumference of the earth.

The oldest bisses date from the 17th and 18th centuries - and people are actually proposing to fill them in and cover them over to make tarmac roads! The enormous scale of the undertaking bears witness to the enterprise, courage and perseverance of our forefathers, as well as their skill and intelligence sharpened by close and unremitting observation of the natural world. The bisses of Valais are part of our national heritage and must not be allowed to die.

At the same press conference, the Valaisan author Maurice Zermatten described the bisses in this way:

'For century after century the bisse has necessarily been a matter of prime concern for the people of our high Rhône valley. With a climate so dry, a soil so poor, and with rock outcropping everywhere, for fifty generations, water has signified life. Without water, no harvest; drought meant misery and death. The bisse is the artery bringing the life-giving element into this great thirsty sunburnt body, our land. The bisse is as old as our agriculture, our mountain paths, our highways, our homes. The very life of our community, especially in the high mountain areas, would simply not have been possible without it.'

The whole way of life of our Valaisan vine-growers and mountain people unrolls like a sort of back-cloth along our bisses. Through larch-timber conduits, channels of rock, canals through the fields and forests, cuttings through glacial moraine, our bisses run everywhere, every which way, and we walk beside them. All through the centuries, people of the land have followed their saving streams, their life-giving presence, hearing the water's small rippling song that promises never to let them down. Rains are so scanty on these dry uplands, and prayers for rain so rarely answered, that the only hope for salvation has floated on these tamed and willing waters. For two or three thousand years, these unfailing and indispensable lifelines have enabled the mountain dwellers of Valais to survive the annual scourge of drought - yet nobody seems distressed to see them disappear.

In 1974, in the book 'Portrait d'un guide, Armand Charlet', Sir Douglas Busk, diplomat, alpinist and writer, wrote... 'The excursion to the Col de Balme, descending eventually towards Switzerland, was very fashionable in the years around 1860 and after. On some days, it was possible to count over a hundred mules waiting at Montenvers, tied up in long lines. Though now served by a rack-railway, Montenvers was just as crowded then as it is today. For intrepid walkers there was also the tour of the Mont-Blanc range, which included crossing four or five high cols following reasonable paths through alpine pastures, and took a week or ten days of unhurried walking. The cost of a guide and mule was then five francs a day - around eighteen francs today.'

### Glaciers in the Val d'Aosta

'The high average altitude of this area, and especially the presence of the three great alpine peaks, Mont-Blanc, Mont Rose and the Grand Paradis, plus a whole host of summits of over 4,000 metres, means that Val d'Aosta experiences heavy snow conditions in 190 square kilometres or 5.9% of its total area. This is more than Tarentaise Maurienne with 4.8% but less than in Valais with 18.2% and 850 square kilometres of glaciers.

There are only a few big ice-fields: the Miage is 1,129 hectares and 10 kilometres long and the Brenva 730 hectares and 6.7 kilometres long. The glacial tongues are rather short, and milky outflows are rare in the Swiss Alps or on the Savoy side of Mont-Blanc.'

The Val d'Aosta glaciers intrude shyly into the valleys; one has to be a climber to see them properly. Glaciers are seldom a popular attraction, but they do not lack interest. The fact that they retain water during the cold season is compensated for by the water they lose in summer thaw which fills the reservoirs, activates the hydro-electric power stations and irrigates the thirsty countryside. During the hot season, with little rainfall, the inhabitants of the Val d'Aosta could not survive without this precious supply of water coming off the high mountains by innumerable streams.

### Plan de l'Au
*1,330m*

2:10

A gentle slope leads up towards the Chalet de la Jure, at the base of the Clochers d'Arpette. Climb to the left among larches in the Vallon de Six-Fours, cross the stream, then after a steep section through hairpin bends, overgrown with bushes, you reach the top of the forest. The path continues on the level, heading northwards across alpine pastures, then bears west to reach the Fermes de Bovine.

### Fermes de Bovine
*1,987m*
*From an alpine pasture here, views of Martigny, the Rhône valley and Valais.*

1:30

### COL DE LA FORCLAZ
🏠 ✗ 🚌
*1,526m*
*Important road pass linking Martigny and Chamonix via la Châtelard, situated between Mont de l'Arpille and Pointe Ronde, of which the rounded shoulder looking down on the pass is called Croix des Prélayes.*

0:30

### LE PEUTY
⌂ ⚠
*1,326m*
*Hamlet which is part of Trient*
**Detour** *10 mins*
### TRIENT
🏠 ⌂ ⚠ ✗ 🚂 🚌 🅿

1:30

### Les Tseppes
*1,932m*
*Typical Valaisan alpine pasture tucked away on a*

0:45

Still on the flat at first, the GR then climbs through meadowland on the mountainside to the Collet Portalo at 2,049 metres. It descends through a larch forest, where the combes give glimpses of Martigny and the road to Col de la Forclaz, and reaches the chalet de la Giète at 1,884 metres. It follows the stream down, descending from one level to another through a forest to Col de la Forclaz.

From the Col de la Forclaz, take the path south west waymarked white-red-white, descending below the main road, crossing underneath it, and over the Trient stream to the hamlet of Le Peuty.

**Detour** Turn right at the junction and go through Le Peuty to reach Trient.

**Junction** The Alternative route to Tré-le-Champ via Vallorcine leaves the TMB at Le Peuty.

**Alternative route** This new route enables walkers to enjoy a varied mountain landscape with beautiful panoramic views; opens up the Vallorcine commune, hitherto ignored by the TMB routes, and provides a means of reaching the Chamonix Valley on foot from Trient. From Le Peuty, take the road north along the stream towards Trient. Do not cross the brook, but just before the bridge, take the good forest path on the left. It rises rapidly, first crossing, and then following hairpin bends up to the pasture of Les Tseppes.

The GR carries on climbing north west to a grassy ridge at 1,996 metres, then turns left around the Pointe de Carraye and runs south south west to the houses of Catogne.

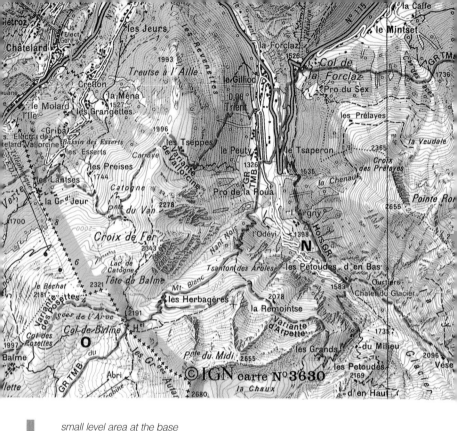

small level area at the base of a cross; Dairy products available.

**Catogne**
*2,011m*
*Shelter if necessary in old cattle sheds.*

**1:00**

The path descends steeply towards the pastures of Les Preises. Passing the deserted cattle sheds of Lantses at 1,730 metres, it continues just below the pastures of La Grand'Jeur and reaches the frontier level.

**Frontier Level**
*1,611m*

**1:00**

Cross diagonally under the cable-car line and take the forest footpath with regular French waymarks, avoiding an old workmen's track on the left. The GR slopes down through the Forêt Verte woods to the village of Vallorcine.

**VALLORCINE**
Ⓗ ⌂ ⚑ ✕ ⛴ 🚌 🚆 🛈
*Church presbytery and the small cemetery in adjacent hamlet of Sizeray are worth seeing, hidden behind a solid wall as protection against avalanches.*

**0:50**

The path comes round to the south of the railway station and passes the Plan de L'Envers, then runs along the valley bottom beside the railway, and along the old stage-coach route, up towards the SNCF station at Buet and La Chapelle des Montets. Climbing gradually, the GR passes the railway tunnel entrance to reach the Col des Montets.

**Le Col des Montets**
*1,461m*

**Warning** The regular GRTMB route between the Col des Montets and the chalet des Chéserys includes a difficult stretch involving the ascent of a rock chimney on the Aiguillette d'Argentière. Walkers lacking mountain experience and those preferring an easier route should take the following short alternative via Les Deviets.

**Alternative route** avoiding l'Aiguille d'Argentière. From the Col des Montets take a path heading south west, climbing steeply up and bending first right and then left to 1,806 metres. Continue south westwards to Les Deviets, and on to join the regular TMB shortly before reaching the Chalet des Chéserys.

0:10

The GR leaves the pass and heads south, taking a short cut to meet the road just before rejoining the regular TMB at the hamlet of Tré-le-Champ.

**TRÉ-LE-CHAMP**

**Junction** The Alternative route via Vallorcine rejoins the GRTMB.

**LE PEUTY**

At Le Peuty the GRTMB turns sharp left, south, and rises among meadows to the Nant Noir stream and crosses it, turns right, along the stream for 100 metres and then left into the forest where the slope becomes steeper, passing Tsanton des Aroles and coming out across the alpine pastures to reach the sheep pens of Les Herbagères.

2:00

**Les Herbagères**
*2,033m*
*Water point slightly to the east of the chalets.*

**Warning** Do not take water from the stream to the west of the chalets: it is used as a sewer by the Chalet-Hotel at the Col de Balme.

The GR continues climbing and comes to a junction.

**Junction** The Alternative via the Fenêtre d'Arpette rejoins the GRTMB.

The GR then passes the Chalet des Grands, and climbs through hairpin bends to the Col de Balme.

**Col de Balme**
*2,191m*

**Junction** The Alternative route via Les Posettes leaves the TMB.

*On the frontier between France and Switzerland; A wide combe on the ridge links Les Grandes Autanes to the Tête de Balme. Splendid views: on Swiss side over the Rhône valley and Bernese Alps, on French side the Chamonix valley, with Mont-Blanc massif on the left, L'Aiguille Verte and Aiguilles de Chamonix in foreground and Les Aiguilles Rouges on the right; Above, and to the left on the French side, upper terminal of chair-lift from Le Tour.*

0:25

**Col des Posettes**
*1,997m*
*Broad col, with beautiful views over the Vallorcine valley, Buet Massif,*

2:00

**Alternative route** from the Col de Balme to Tré-le-Champ via the Col des Posettes. This beautiful alternative route, opened in 1975 by the Mountain Paths Commission of Chamonix, is specially recommended as taking walkers through a rather more stark and rugged landscape, with unrestricted views of the Mont-Blanc massif, and, at the Col des Posettes, of Le Buet and the Vallorcine valley. It also keeps out of sight of the Balme-Charamillon ski lifts. At Col de Balme, take the path running westwards across the mountain side, which comes from the alpine pastures of Balme. In a combe on the left are the sources of the river Arve, and higher up, on the right, north, is the site of the Plan des Reines, or 'Queens' meadow.

The GR passes to the south of Béchat and then descends south-westwards to the Col des Posettes.

The GR heads south west above the Chalets de Balme, and climbs up towards the ridge leading to L'Aiguillette des Posettes at 2,201 metres. By way of the ridge of Frettes and the Tête de Chenavier at 1,927 metres the GR

---

**'Queens' Meadow'**

This was where local cattle farmers customarily held their famous cow fights. It must be emphasised that mountain cows have an innate love of fighting, deriving from the instinctively hierarchical social organisation, or 'pecking order', within the herd, where the strongest animal is 'queen'.

The periodical '13 Etoiles' recently quoted an article by one Louis Courthion which appeared in the 'Confédéré' of 17 August 1917, describing an advertisement one of the Chamonix valley farmers had placed in the local Martigny newspaper on 4 August: 'To all queen enthusiasts! The owner of Charamillon's mountain queen challenges the owners of all neighbouring mountain queens to a cow fight at the Col de Balme on any day they please.'

The Swiss, defied in this way, were not slow to rise to the defence of their time-honoured traditions. On 15 August, the same newspaper carried this dignified response: 'To all queen enthusiasts! M. August Farquet takes up the challenge issued in the Confédéré of 4 August. His queen, standing firm at the frontier on her hocks of steel, is ready to take on any cow in the neighbourhood. She fears none, and will be there on Sunday 19 August, at 2 in the afternoon, at the Col de Balme.'

Let us hope that M. August Farquet's queen will defend herself well on Sunday, and put paid to our neighbours' hopes of depriving Valais of a supremacy never before contested... End of quote.

*Emosson lakes and the peaks of the Mont-Blanc massif.*

## TRÉ-LE-CHAMP
⌂
*1,417m*
**Detour,**
**ARGENTIÈRE**
Ⓗ ⌂ ⛺ ✗ 🚊 🚌 🚃
*1,250m*
*Village some 1,500 metres to the south on Chamonix road.*

## Col de Balme
*2,191m*

2:00

## LE TOUR
Ⓗ ⛺ ✗ 🚃
*1,463m*
*First village of the Chamonix valley, as you come from the north east; A summer and winter resort, dominated by the foot of the Glacier du Tour; Chairlift to Charamillon and Balme.*

0:15

## MONTROC-LE-PLANET
Ⓗ 🚌 🚃
**Detour** *5 mins*
## LES FRASSERANDS
⌂
*1,360m*

0:20

## TRÉ-LE-CHAMP
⌂
*1,417m*

comes down through meadows and then woodland to rejoin the regular TMB at Tré-le-Champ.

**Junction** The Alternative route via the Col des Posettes rejoins the GRTMB.

**Detour** You can either walk along the road, or take a shuttle bus or train from Montroc-le-Planet.

**Important** At the Col de Balme the waymarking reverts to the white and red of the regular GRTMB.

**Note** The regular GRTMB goes down from the Col de Balme across alpine pastures, passing the Chalets de Charamillon on the left, to the east, and on the right, the station of the chairlift from Le Tour. The path continues down, sometimes obscured by ski-runs or sheep tracks, and finally arrives at the village of Le Tour.

The TMB follows the road down for 1 kilometre to the SNCF station at Montroc-le-Planet.

**Detour** Continue along the road to les Frasserands. In front of the SNCF station, the GR bends right, then turns immediately left to cross the railway at the tunnel entrance - often in winter the only means of access to Vallorcine. Follow a path winding through woods, then fields, where you turn right to reach the hamlet of Tré-le-Champ.

**Junction** The 2 Alternative routes, from Le Peuty via Vallorcine and from the Col de Balme via the Col des Posettes, both join the regular TMB.

**Warning** Walkers lacking mountain experience and those wanting to avoid the more difficult

ascent of l'Aiguillette d'Argentière on the regular TMB, should take the short alternative via Les Deviets.

**Alternative route** via Les Deviets avoiding l'Aiguillette d'Argentière. From Tré-le-Champ climb north on the road towards the Col des Montets. Ignore the alternative route from the Col des Posettes on the right, and shortly after it, take the rising path to the left, north west, to meet the path coming from the Col des Montets. Turn left, westwards, along the path, and climb steeply up through bends to 1,806 metres. Continue south west to Les Deviets, and on to rejoin the regular TMB just before the Chalet des Chéserys.

2:45

---

### Nature reserve of Les Aiguilles Rouges

This reserve was created in 1974. It comprises 3,500 hectares in the Chamonix and Vallorcine communes, and includes the whole Aiguilles Rouges massif from the Col des Montets in the north east to the Col du Brévent in the south west, as well as an important part of the 12,500 hectare game reserve of Arve-Giffre. Eventually, perhaps, it will extend to the shores of Lake Geneva. This reserve is the first of a series of newly designated 'general' reserves which will cover very large areas and be less strictly regulated than the traditional reserves. The region is a very popular one for walkers, and you are earnestly requested to respect its regulations.

---

In the hamlet of Tré-le-Champ, the regular GRTMB crosses the road leading to the Col des Montets just below three shepherds' huts on to a path running along a ledge to the south west with unique views of the French side of Mont-Blanc. The path slants up through a sparse wood, and passes the Aiguillette d'Argentière, used by a climbing school.

**Warning** Shortly afterwards, you will have to climb up through wide rock chimneys; ascend with great caution, overhang extending for twenty metres, equipped with cables to provide hand-holds.

The TMB climbs on up and reaches a crossroads. Straight ahead a path leads to the Chalet du Lac Blanc, within 1 hour's walking distance, with restaurant. To the right and slightly above, is the alternative GR from the Col des

Montets which avoids the difficult passage via the Aiguillette d'Argentière. Turning left the GRTMB follows a path descending to the Chalet des Chéserys.

### Chalet des Chéserys

*2,005m*

*Here the GR reaches the so-called 'Plan des Aiguilles Rouges': a long overhang with magnificent views of the complete Mont-Blanc range and its glaciers. Straight in front as you look south east is the Glacier d'Argentière, to its left is the beautiful Aiguille d'Argentière with the Aiguille du Chardonnet in front of it; on the right is the Aiguille Verte, and les Drus looking down on the Mer de Glace.*

1:10

Take the path behind the chalet, not the one below that goes down to Argentière. Cross a few little streams flowing down from Lac Blanc, and after a gentle descending slope, reach the cow sheds and cable-car station of La Flégère.

### CABLE-CAR STATION OF LA FLÉGÈRE
⌂ ✕

*1,875m*

*Orientation table; Views of the Mer de Glace with les Grandes Jorasses on the horizon.*

*In this area a number of excursions are possible: to Lac Blanc (1hr), Argentière (2hrs), la Joux (1hr 45 mins), les Tines (1 hr 30 mins) les Praz (1hr 45 mins).*

*Beginning of the 'Balcon de la Flégère', with views of the Aiguilles de Chamonix.*

0:50

After the cable-car station, you come to a stairway cut in the rock, taking you down to a footpath across pastures. Follow this to the ruined Chalet de Charlanon.

### Ruined Chalet de Charlanon

*1,812m*

*From or near this point, there are paths to Les Praz (1hr 30 mins), Chamonix (2hrs) and to Lac Cornu (2 hrs).*

0:50

The path rises again, crosses La Montagne de la Parsa, and curves around to the back of the old 'Hôtel 2000' at Planpraz where a path leads off on the right to Lac Cornu.

### PLANPRAZ
✕ 🍸

*2,000m*

The GR turns sharp right, behind the old Hôtel 2000, and climbs again, ignoring a path to the right, half way up, leading off to the Pointe des

113

**1:00**

*Intermediate cable-car station for Chamonix-le-Brévent.*
*From or near this point there are paths to Chamonix via the plan des Chablettes (1hr 30 mins), to the Col de Brévent and Lac Cornu within 2 hrs 15 mins, and also to Brévent by way of a chimney within 1 hr 45 mins.*

Vioz. After a few hairpin bends, it reaches the Col du Brévent.

**1:10**

### Col du Brévent
*2,368m*
*Magnificent panorama of the Mont-Blanc range and the Chamonix valley, and looking behind you, the Rochers des Fiz, to the north west, and to the right, the Col d'Anterne.*

**Junction** Here the GRTMB is joined by the GR5 coming in on the right from Lake Geneva. From the Col du Brévent back to Les Houches - and on to the refuge at the Col de la Croix-du-Bonhomme and Les Chapieux, the GRTMB and the GR5 follow the same route.

From the Col du Brévent the GR5 and GRTMB head south west along the northern slopes of Le Brévent, where there are views over the Diose valley with the Rochers des Fiz on the horizon, and often patches of snow still lying in summer, then climb round southwards to the summit.

**0:40**

### Summit of Brévent
*2,526m*
*An easy summit to reach, Brévent is the best viewpoint for Mont-Blanc, from which one can see the whole development of the big Bossons and Taconna glaciers, as well as the climbing routes up to the highest summit in Europe; Orientation table; Upper terminal of cable-cars from Chamonix. New cable lift installed 1988.*

The path goes down over scree with beautiful views over the Lac du Brévent below, then follows the south west spur of Brévent, where there are further views of the Mont-Blanc range.

Ignore a path on the right going to Aiguillette des Houches, just before you arrive at Bellachat.

**0:45**

### BELLACHAT
⌂ ✕
*2,151m*
**Detour** *2 hrs 30 mins*
### CHAMONIX-MONT-BLANC
⌂ ⌂ Å ✕ ⍨ ⛾ ➿ ➿
⚡

The GR descends rapidly through a series of bends, cuts across the Vouillouds ravine and runs through a magnificent conifer forest. After passing the hamlet of Merlet, cross the La Pra ravine and a few metres farther on turn sharp left, out of the forest, and continue along the fence of the Merlet animal reserve.

1,010m
Cable lift terminus.
From Bellachat take the
footpath going down
eastwards, passing Plan-
Lachat.

## MERLET
Ⓗ
1,562m
**Detour** 30 mins
**Chalet-Hôtel de
l'Aiguillette**

0:30

### Statue du Christ-Roi
1,268m
Concrete statue of Christ the
King, work of the sculptor
Serraz, 17 metres high, set
on a 6 metres high plinth
which houses a chapel.

0:30

## LES HOUCHES
Ⓗ Å ✗ ⏱ ⚏ 🚌 🚃 🛈
1,008m
(see map ref 19)
A pleasant village, long and
narrow at the foot of l'Aiguille
du Goûter, where Mont-
Blanc country starts; Its
church has a strange
bulbous steeple, and an
18th century retable. The
viaduct of Saint-Marie, 52
metres high and gorges of
La Diose near Servoz, are
within reach. Museum of
rural and mountain life.

**Detour** To reach the hotel, skirt round the reserve and take a footpath leading towards the Plan de la Cry-Coupeau, at first running along the mountain side and then becoming quite steep and passing below Le Lac Noir. Do not take any of the tracks to the right.

The GR then takes the gravel road around the park, leaving it before long and taking a path through the forest. Look out for waymarks painted on trees by the Forests Department, a wide white line with thin red lines in the middle and at each end. The path winds down through hairpin bends to reach the Christ-Roi statue.

The path continues down, leaves the forest and reaches a kind of esplanade where you immediately turn left on to a path going straight down and cutting across three bends in the tarmac road that goes up to Coupeau. The path reaches the EDF dam on the River Arve, where you turn right, and after a short descent, reach the SNCF station at Les Houches.

# WALK 3

## Tour de la Vanoise

### LES CHAPIEUX
ⓗ ⌂ ⩍ ✕ ⚒

*1,554m*
*Les Chapieux is 18
kilometres from Bourg-Saint-
Maurice on the main N202
road.*

**0:40**

The GRTMB follows a well marked country road,
made up from old shortcuts, to the Chalets de
la Raja.

### Chalets de la Raja
⌂

*1,689m*
*High mountain chalets
normally inhabited in
summertime; motor road
from Les Chapieux ends at
this point.*

**0:40**

The GR follows a path up into the mountain
pastures to the Chalets de Plan Vararo.

### Chalets de Plan Vararo
*2,013m*

**1:25**

The path continues to climb, first through
pastureland and then over rocky slopes,
passing close to a ruined military shelter, to
reach the Refuge of the Col de la Croix-du-
Bonhomme.

### REFUGE DU COL DE LA CROIX-DU-BONHOMME
⌂

*2,443m*
*There is an orientation table;
views over Le Beaufortain
and La Tarentaise.*

**0:10**

The path climbs for a short distance to the Col
de la Croix-du-Bonhomme.

### Col de la Croix-du-Bonhomme
*2,483m*
*This is not in fact the true
Croix-du-Bonhomme pass,
which lies beyond the
refuge to the south, at
2,412m, as shown on IGN
maps; before the 1939-
1945 war a Michelin*

**Junction** The GRTMB joins the GR5 from the
Chamoix valley to the north, and the TMB
alternative route from La Ville des Glaciers via
the Col des Fours.

The route now follows the GR5. It goes slightly
downhill to the south west, passes hard by a
ruined shelter, then climbs to the first spur of
the Crête des Gittes, where you will see a war
memorial.

### The Roselend Dam

This major dam holds in 187 million cubic metres of water covering a surface area of 320 hectares. It is sited on the Doron de Beaufort where the stream passes the granite spur of the Méraillet. Because the glacial action was so uneven, leaving a sharp drop on the left bank and a gently sloping spur on the right, the engineers adopted an original approach resulting in an elegant structure. The closure is effected by a buttressed dam which, in crossing the deep gorge of the Doron, is supported on a great arch cut off at a 45° angle, a principle used in the great viaducts. Rising 150 metres from the bottom of the gorge and spanning a breadth of 804 metres, the dam required 950,000 cubic metres of concrete in its construction.

*waymarker was sited here, claiming this to be the pass, and the error has stuck.*

**1:10**

*War memorial erected in memory of soldiers of the alpine regiments who, to make it invisible from the Col de la Seigne, carved out a military road on the north face of the mountain.*

The path, clearly marked in the broken schists, climbs to the foot of the northern summit of the Gittes, then crosses to the southern slope and returns to the northern side at the foot of the southern summit.

**Warning** The path continues on the north-facing slope which is very steep, especially above the Col de la Sauce; when the path is still blocked, it is easier to follow the line of the crest which is often clear of snow.

The path now descends to the Col de la Sauce.

### Col de la Sauce

*2,306m*
*(see map ref A)*
*Fine views over the Col du Bonhomme to the north and the Aiguille du Grand-Fond to the south; purple gentians growing, but do not pick them.*

**0:45**

The GR5 continues its descent, passing close to a chalet called 'Bel Air' where dairy products are obtainable. Carry on down the east side of the Roc au Vent and taking the CAF hostel, a former roadmender's house, as your reference point, you will arrive at Plan de la Lai.

### PLAN DE LA LAI

⌂
*1,815m*
*The GR is crossed by the D217 road, and runs very close to the artificial lake created by the Roselend dam.*

**0:45**

At the Plan de la Lai refuge, follow the road for 100 metres in a westerly direction, then turn left on to a cart track leading uphill towards a new chalet. At the end of the made up road, take the badly waymarked path opposite in the meadow. Follow it southwards into the little valley between the escarpments overlooking the Lac de Roselend on the right and the first spurs of the Grand-Fond chain. You will come to the foot of a fairly steep slope covered in rhododendron bushes. Clearly visible here, the path winds its way up to the top and comes out into a meadow at the Chalet de Petite Berge.

### Chalet de Petite Berge

*2,071m*
*(see map ref B)*
*Fine view over Le Beaufortain and surrounding areas and the dam.*

**0:20**

Looking south west, on a rise at the end of the vast hollow of pastureland, you will see the Chalet of the Grande-Berge, the next landmark on the route. Having got your bearings, take whichever way you fancy to reach it. The path is officially waymarked on the mountainside to the left, though it is not easy to follow as it goes through marshland and over boggy ground.

## Chalet de Grande Berge
*2,055m*

The GR drops almost imperceptibly along the mountain side, crosses an area of marshy ground in the direction of 3 summer chalets, and reaches a point above the hamlet of Treicol. The path crosses a mountain stream, rises to the foot of the Treicol waterfalls and there joins a pathway coming from the Lac de Roselend and Treicol. As you climb up through the scree and rocks, you will ford a mountain stream descending from a fine waterfall though the crossing may be difficult if it has been raining hard. Clambering over the slopes on the right bank of the Treicol stream, you emerge into meadowland.

**1:00**

## Chalet de Presset
*2,011m*
*(see map ref C)*
*Situated close to the junction with the pathway leading to the Col du Coin.*

From the Chalet de Presset, the GR5 turns eastward, leaving the path leading to the Chalet and Col du Coin on the right hand side. You can make out the gap of the pass to the south.

**Warning** When there is still snow on the ground, the pathway up to the Col du Bresson is not easy to distinguish.

**1:30**

Continuing eastward, you ascend a narrow valley, avoiding boulders, until you reach the Col de Bresson.

### 'Le Versant du Soleil'
#### The south-facing valley-side

One might think that the area falling away southwards towards La Tarantaise did not merit a section of its own. Nevertheless, 3 communes, La Côte d'Aime, Granier and Valezan, known collectively as Le Versant du Soleil, lie hereabouts. More exposed to the sun and so less favoured by the snow, they have not become ski resorts like the villages on the other side of the valley. For years their main activity was agriculture, but as farming declined, so did the population of the area. Now other occupations have emerged; first a combination of agriculture and industry, then agriculture combined with tourism. In winter, the young people cross to the other side!

The 3 communes have joined forces to fight their decline. In common with others they are making plans to accommodate walkers and long-distance skiers and improving the facilities they can offer. Soon it will be possible to enjoy some fine walking off the beaten track in this area.

### Col de Bresson
*2,469m*
*From the col there are breathtaking views of the nearby monolithic Pierre Menta to the south, reminiscent of the Dolomites, and of Mont Pourri to the south east.*

1:00

**Detour** *20 mins*
### REFUGE DE PRESSET
⌂
*2,514m*
*Situated, sheltered from avalanches, on a mound above the Lac de Presset and facing the vertical walls of La Pierre Menta.*

### CHALET DE LA BALME
⌂
*2,009m*
*(see map ref D)*

2:30

**Detour** To reach the refuge, go down from the Col de Bresson taking a faintly defined path on your left to the north east.

From the Col de Bresson the path leads downhill through pastures crisscrossed by cattle tracks. Pay close attention to the waymarks. Carry on down the course of the Ormente until you reach the Chalet de la Balme.

After the Chalet de la Balme, first go downhill in a north-easterly direction, leaving on your left, and, due north, the combe rising towards the Col de la Nova. The GR5 then turns southwards and follows the left bank of the Ormente down into the valley. When you come in view of the Laval chalets, do not cross the stream but continue on the left bank so as to avoid the new road. You will soon reach some recently constructed sheep pens, opposite the hamlet of Foran on the other bank. Carry on down the valley walking parallel with the Valezan irrigation canal (2 other such canals serve Les Chapelles and La Côte d'Aime). The path leads on to the Chalets des Fours and there joins a motor road to Valezan.

## VALEZAN
⌂
*1,186m*
*Picturesque village, typical of La Tarentaise; houses at different levels; main street follows the line of steepest slope; the church has an 18th century altar-piece.*

0:45

The GR5 continues downwards via Rocheray and Le Crey to the village of Bellentre.

## BELLENTRE
⌂ Å ✕ ⛴ ▭
*776m*
*Situated on the N90 in the Isère valley; church has works of art dating from 17th and 18th centuries; the belfry was restored in 1971, but after difficulty in finding suitable materials it was roofed with galvanised iron; since covered with stainless steel to retain its former brilliance.*

0:45

Walk through the village, crossing the N90 and take the road down to the Isère. Cross the river by the bridge and turn left, and to the east, following the road as far as Landry.

## LANDRY
⌂ Å ✕ ⛴ ▭ ⛟
*777m*
*(see map ref E)*
*Lies on the left bank of the Isère between Bellentre and Bourg-St-Maurice. The Peisey-Nancroix valley starts from here; church has a 17th century reredos and a beam bearing the crucifix, above which angels hover, collecting the blood of Christ..*

1:30

From Landry the GR5 begins to ascend the Peisey valley. Follow the D87 for a short distance, taking the short cuts which avoid the hairpin bends in the road. When you rejoin the road for the third time, at a height of 1,100 metres, follow it for a little way, then take the path which brings you down to the course of the Ponturin. Follow the stream as far as the hamlet of Le Moulin.

## Le Moulin
*1,264m*
*(see map ref F)*
*From here the village of Peisey is only a few minutes away.*

From the hamlet of Le Moulin, walk down to and cross the Ponturin, then follow the left bank as far as the bridge called Pont Romano.

125

© IGN carte Nº 3
3

## La Tarentaise

Since the beginning of the century, this part of Savoy has probably experienced more sweeping changes than any other. In a few decades it has 'progressed' from mule transport to helicopters and, in places, the 2 ways of life exist side by side. There has been a price to pay for such a transformation, by both the natural environment and its inhabitants.

In the past, the region was intensively farmed, despite the harsh climate: pocket-handkerchief fields of rye would be reaped just before the first snowfall and the grain laid out to continue ripening on people's balconies. Large herds of tarine cows would be driven up to their summer pastures, up to their shoulders in the mud, as soon as the snow had melted. From their milk Beaufort, a rich mountain cheese, was made, and still is today. Small-scale industry and some tourism enabled this valley to survive.

Today, this area is one of the biggest skiing centres in the world, with huge resorts conceived as part of 'Plan Neige' - a winter sports development project. Gigantic towers and huge pylons carry a spider's web of ski lift cables. The region also produces a large amount of hydro-electricity, generated from the impressive Tignes dam.

For tomorrow, new dams may well cause the people and their environment further strain and stress. If completed, one such project would inundate several hectares of the National Park near the commune of Sainte-Foy. In the future, if prospecting is successful, La Tarentaise may become a major producer of uranium.

Will this valley, with its rich natural and cultural heritage, be able to keep its character intact? Will its people be able to control the process of change now taking place? In the past they survived through extraordinary tenacity, courage and patience. Maybe these qualities will again enable them to make their voice heard and ensure that acceptable and necessary development does not bring with it the irreversible destruction of their heritage.

There is a tradition of emigration among the people of La Tarentaise. This account written by the Curé Savarin in 1869 speaks of an object in the local church donated by one such emigrant:

'Jean-François Cléaz started as a pedlar, became a successful merchant, married Maria Oswaldin, a rich heiress from Augsburg, and ended his career as official purveyor to His Majesty Leopold 1st, Archduke of Austria, King of Hungary and Bohemia.... In 1685 he had a magnificent monstrance made for his home church at Bellentre; it was sculpted in solid silver and set with precious stones of different colours. The inside of the base bears the following inscription: "I, Jean-François-Cléaz, from the poor end of Bellentre, merchant and burger of Augsburg, donate this vessel to my patron, Saint Andrew." He still considered himself a good parishioner of Saint-André de Bellentre, despite his social success in far-away Bavaria!'

Walkers interested in the history of this valley may like to read *Une vieille vallée raconte ses souvenirs:* a short history of the Tarentaise by Yves Brêche and Lucien Chavoutier, Collection Trésors de la Savoie, BP 29, 73230 Saint-Alban.

The GR5 runs through one of the most beautiful neighbouring valleys, Peisey Nancroix, but if you feel like exploring Tarentaise more fully before moving on, you might like to investigate another valley which has retained all its charm, Champagny-en-Vanoise.

Start from the village of Sainte-Foy-en-Tarentaise for one of the most beautiful walks in the whole of Savoy, especially in the autumn. From the hamlet of La Raie, upstream from the village of La Thuile, climb the valley side towards Le Chenal and Le Fenil. From here, a path leads to the impressive hamlet of Le Monal where a track goes on via Bon Conseil to La Masure and Le Miroir. These hamlets, especially Le Miroir and Le Monal, are typical of the picturesque local architecture, combining wood and stone. In the autumn, the larches, now golden, are mirrored in the many small lakes, investing Le Monal with a special beauty against the breathtaking north face of Mont Pourri.

On the other, the National Park side of the valley, the climb up to the Refuge de Turia or the Refuge de la Martin via La Gurraz, provides a good chance of seeing chamois in abundance and of enjoying a fine view of the Grande Sassière massifs and even of Mont Blanc.

**The National Park refuge de Turia** - 2,400 metres, accommodates 24, no warden, 2 hours from La Gurraz, sleeping and cooking facilities.
**The National Park refuge de la Martin** - 2,150 metres, accommodates 34, no warden, 2 hours from La Gurraz, sleeping and cooking facilities.

These 2 refuges are strategically placed on the 'Tour of Mont Pourri', which follows the route: Rosuel, Col de la Sachette, La Martin, Arcs 2,000, Col de la Chal, Refuge du Mont Pourri.

The GR is about to enter the Vanoise National Park; walkers should make a careful study of the Notice to Visitors (see page 132).

Walkers will have the opportunity of observing all the different stages of mountain vegetation and animal life, as well as the varied geological structure of the Vanoise.

For each stretch of the nature trail, a description of the natural environment has been prepared by M. Claude Garti, with the assistance of 2 National Park rangers, Henri Flandin and Régis Villibord, who are based at Peisey-Nancroix.

pic noir

## From Landry to Moulin

As far as Moulin, the Ponturin valley has a floor of schists and sandstones from the carboniferous period. At first the GR runs along at the foothill level, up to the 975 metres mark. Here the riverside forest consists of deciduous trees requiring a rich, deep, well-watered soil. Ash and hazel abound, in the company of the common pedunculate oak, aspen, walnut and sycamore. Beside the stream grow alder, birch, sallow willow and buckthorn, and farther up the valley, field maple. Damp-loving herbaceous plants such as herb robert and wood cranesbill, meadow vetchling and wild sage are found in close association with dry meadow species, such as yarrow, coronilla, wormwood, savory and wild marjoram, which grow on the quickly-draining sandy alluvial deposits, while sun-loving rosebay willowherb and white mullein brighten the wayside verges. We cannot list all the animal species to be found at this altitude, but they are little different from those of the plains and lower hillsides.

Only above 975 metres, where the climate is cooler and damper, does the true mountain vegetation and fauna begin. The first level is characterized by mixed woodland of spruce and hazel, interspersed with field maple, sycamore, ash, aspen, service tree, rowan and larch.

Yellow and large-flowered foxgloves and peach-leaved campanula are typical of the woodland undergrowth, where red hare's lettuce, wall lettuce, speedwell and broad-leaved willowherb are also found. Other plants show the presence of lime in the soil: broad helleborine, wild columbine, greater astrantia, mountain knapweed and wood cow-wheat.

In the forest there sounds the cascading song of the chaffinch, a seed-eating bird with a short, stout beak like the bullfinch and crossbill which frequent the highland coniferous woods. The song thrush lives in the same sort of habitat, but has a long, pointed beak, and so does the robin. Because of its repeated call note, the chiffchaff is often known as the 'water counter', a small insect-eater with a delicate bill, like the blackcap and garden warbler, which also thrive in the undergrowth. The tits, with their short beaks and acrobatic habits, prefer areas of mixed woodland; the great tit, largest and most widespread of the family, and the blue and long-tailed tits. Sometimes you will hear the harsh cry of a jay among the oaks, the 'laugh' of the 'yaffle' or green woodpecker and the drumming of the black and the great spotted woodpeckers, while buzzards and sparrowhawks hunt on the woodland margins.

Above 1,220 metres the forest has been cleared to make way for fairly dry hay meadows of tall oat-grass, mingling with brome-grass, quaking grass, sainfoin and meadow sage. Near the hamlet of Lanches, the meadowland has been taken over by a stand of young larches. The whinchat is the commonest bird in these mountain pastures, while the citril finch frequents the woodland fringes.

## From Moulin to Rosuel

After Moulin we enter an area of metamorphic rocks. The gneisses of Bellcôte and Mont Pourri overthrust a band of gypsum and ochre-coloured dolomitic limestone full of caves, and clearly visible between Les Lanches and Rosuel. The valley cross-section broadens out and becomes U-shaped, an indication of its glacial origin. A step formation joins the hanging glacial valleys of Nant Bénin and Ponturin. Small residues of perpetual ice remain in the cirque of Bellcôte.

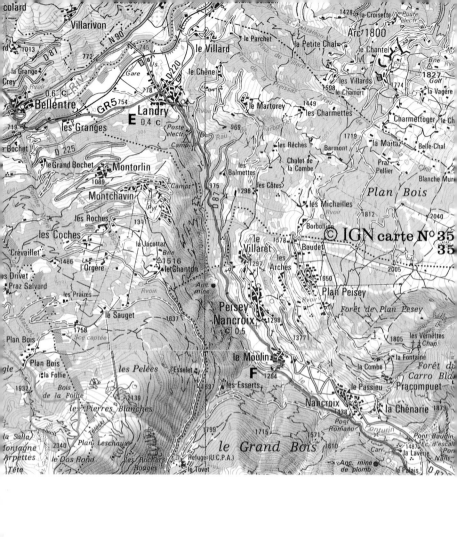

130

**Detour**
**PEISEY**

🏠 🏘 🍴 🚠 🛈

0:15

*1,298m*
*Take the D87 from Le*
*Moulin, turning left.*

**Pont Romano**
*1,438m*
**Detour**
**NANCROIX**

🏠 🚠

0:45

*Cross the bridge over the*
*Ponturin.*

The GR5 continues along the left bank, passing the reception building of the camp site at Glières where there is a school for cross-country skiing. Close by, the path joins a forest track leading to the 'Palais de la Mine', the first mining school, founded by Napoleon 1st. Continue along a farm track, then cross the D87 to reach the hamlet of Les Lanches.

### Beaufort, a great cheese from Savoy

Beaufort is a mountain cheese, rather like gruyère, made in the alpine regions of Savoy: the Beaufortin at the foot of Mont Blanc, and the Maurienne and Tarentaise areas, which include the Vanoise National Park.

These regions are renowned for their vast tracts of pasture land, where herds of golden-brown tarine cows graze at altitudes up to 2,500 metres and higher.

It was in these mountain pastures that, in times past, the ancient methods of making and maturing Beaufort cheese were brought to perfection. And so it came to be known for its nutty, full-bodied flavour, which derives from the extraordinary richness of the flora in the uncultivated meadows of these alpine valleys, in their setting of snow-clad peaks.

A Beaufort cheese has the form of a flat millstone with slightly curved sides weighing between 30 and 40 kilogrammes, and when fully matured is a reddish brown colour.

Inside, the cheese is rich, firm, flexible and tasty, almost without holes, but with a thready texture to it.

Making Beaufort is a demanding business. Only natural full-cream milk from the region can be used, and it must be of high bacteriological purity - in short, only milk of the highest quality.

Although in summertime some cheese is still made in the mountain chalets, nowadays the milk from each farm or pasture is generally collected morning and evening and brought down to a local cheese factory where more modern equipment is used.

Following the traditional practice, the milk is meticulously transformed into curds, then cut up and worked into fine flakes. After heating to different temperatures, the curds are pressed in beechwood moulds to give the cheese its final shape and let the famous crust form.

Each mould is numbered 24 hours later, passed through a bath of brine and stacked on shelves in cellars where it will mature for over 6 months, each cheese being carefully tended and watched over, until the day when experts will come to test, grade and pack it. Only then will it be sent forth into the world, a delectable, nourishing food.

Chief product of the local mountain agriculture, Beaufort remains today one of the few regional cheeses to come from a single rural area. Natural and rich in flavour, it is truly a noble food, by virtue of its hand-made quality.

This passage was kindly contributed by Maxime Viallet, farmer and President of the Co-opérative laitière de Beaufortin at Beaufort-sur-Doron.

### Vanoise National Park
#### *Notice to visitors*

Although the paths set aside for walkers in the Vanoise National Park do not present any special difficulties, it should be remembered that some sections of most of them are at high altitude, where a sudden change in the weather can spell real danger for visitors and ramblers unused to mountain conditions.

It is accordingly strongly recommended:

1. That no one on any account sets out on a mountain excursion, even in fine weather, without suitable equipment:
- strong walking shoes which come up over the ankle (not boots);
- an anorak or waterproof garment;
- sun glasses;
- a rucksack and provisions, etc.

2. That no one undertakes excursions beyond the strength of any member of the party, particularly children.

3. That no one sets off alone, nor leaves the beaten track, unless a trained mountaineer and familiar with the massif.

4. That the services of an officially qualified guide are used for any excursions over rocky terrain and glaciers, and of a suitably qualified person, for walks on footpaths and grassy areas at lower altitudes.

### Visitors, walkers, friends,

This National Park, established for you and future generations, cannot be safeguarded without your cooperation.

There are special regulations which forbid hunting and govern fishing, grazing, forestry and public access.

We request you:
- to follow paths and not take short cuts across hairpin bends;
- not to pick or remove flowers, fruits or rock samples;
- not to disturb the peace of the park by making excessive noise, shouting or playing audio equipment;
- not to bring a dog into the park, even on a lead;
- to take your rubbish away with you when you have used a refuge;
- not to camp or sleep out;
- not to light fires.

These regulations are laid down in the Decree of 6 July 1963 establishing the National Park.

The preservation of this area and visitors' enjoyment of it depend on your observing these rules.

## IN SAVOY
### *A high-mountain national park*

The Vanoise National Park was established in 1963. It covers an area of 53,000 hectares, all within the Département de la Savoie, between the high valleys of the Arc (Maurienne) and the Isère (Tarentaise) and as far as the Italian frontier where, for about 7 kilometres, it borders the Italian Gran Paradiso National Park.

About 100 years ago, the last pairs of alpine ibex, which had taken refuge in the Italian Gran Paradiso massif, were saved from total extinction by the efforts of the 'huntsman king', Victor Emmanuel II. On 3 December 1922, his royal hunting grounds were set aside as a national park. The need, 40 years later, to ensure the survival of this species on the French side of the Alps led to the creation of the Vanoise National Park. Like the Gran Paradiso, it extends over a high mountain area ranging from altitudes of 1,250 to 3,852 metres -

the summit of La Grande Casse. Although extremely rugged, with 107 peaks over 3,000 metres, the massif is divided by deep, verdant valleys, which are interconnected by many easily accessible mountain passes.

In addition to the grandiose beauty of its alpine scenery, the Vanoise is of exceptional interest for its complex geological features (rocks include crystalline sandstones, limestones, gypsums and gneiss), the wide range of altitude within the massif, and its strategic position as a meeting place of alpine cultures.

### Les Lanches
*1,523m*

0:10

Go through the hamlet and join the old road by crossing the Ponturin, then continue as far as the hamlet of Les Bettières. There, recross the stream and you will come to the Refuge de la Porte du Parc de Rosuel.

### PORTE DU PARC DE ROSUEL
⌂ ✕

*1,556m*
*(see map ref G)*
*The architecture of this so-called 'gate', a refuge owned by the Vanoise National Park, is a happy marriage between the use of traditional building materials and the modern look given by a wave-shaped roof of growing grass. The roof was designed to allow an avalanche to flow over the building without destroying it.*

*Blocks of gneiss and limestone are widely scattered over the meadows. On the opposite side of the valley, you can make out the intakes of 3 big waterfalls which, together with the Ponturin, feed the Lac de Chevril through an 8 kilometre tunnel.*

1:30

After the Porte du Parc de Rosuel refuge, the GR5 leaves the track to Gurraz on the left and continues up over the alluvial cone of the Aliet.

Next, cross a scrubby area of green alders until you come to a larch forest. From here you have an excellent view down the valley of Peisey to the south-eastern slopes of Le Beaufortin at its opening. This valley once experienced a period of great prosperity, due to its lead and silver mines and bell foundries. Once out of the forest, you begin to ascend a steeper slope. This is in fact a sill of gneiss. The rock is polished and scored lengthwise, a sign of glacial erosion. The GR5 crosses the Ponturin one last time by a bridge at a spot known as 'Les Pertes du Ponturin'. In fact the stream disappears here among loose limestone blocks brought down from the Aliet by the glacier. A final climb brings you to the Chalet du Berthoud.

### Chalet du Berthoud
*2,091m*
*Chalet used by the local National Park rangers and saves them the trouble of*

The path keeps to the right bank of the stream as far as the Chalets de la Plagne.

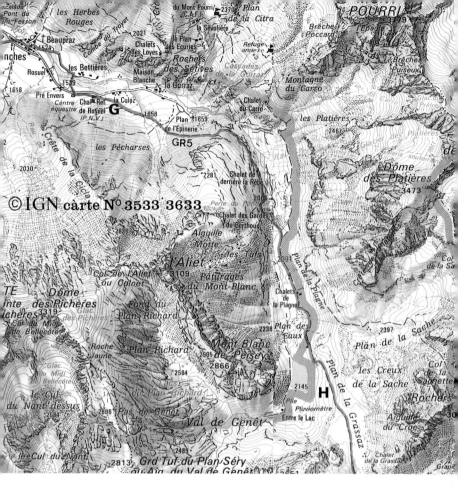

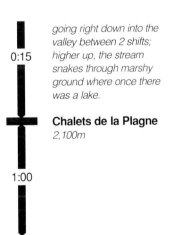

going right down into the valley between 2 shifts; higher up, the stream snakes through marshy ground where once there was a lake.

**0:15**

### Chalets de la Plagne
*2,100m*

**1:00**

From Chalets de la Plagne, the GR continues upwards, leaving the path to Col de la Sachette on the left. Gradually the Lac de la Plagne (see map ref H) comes into full view. On your right, you will see a track leading to the Col de la Grassaz, before you reach the ruins of the Chalet de la Grassaz.

### From Rosuel to Chalets de la Plagne

Our nature trail now enters the upper mountain level in the outer zone of the Park, passing through the last hay meadows characterised by yellow oat-grass. In its company grow snakeweed, globe flower, goat's-beard and yellow hop trefoil, and also the pink 'red' clover and white mountain clover. The violet flowers of wood crane's-bill, field gentian, self-heal and small scabious are interspersed with the white of yarrow and grass of parnassus. Among limestone rocks the milk vetch, mountain vetch and small cypress spurge flourish, while Fleischer's willowherb thrives on silicious terrain. Especially vigorous here are the plants which the sheep and cattle avoid: stemless and carline thistles, and the poisonous white false hellebore. Higher still, the meadows give way to moorland, covered in a shrubby growth of larch and birch, and bushes of spring buckthorn.

At 1,760 metres we enter the sub-alpine level, marked in this locality by thickets of green alder. The shrubby formation is very thick on the north-west facing slopes, less sunny and damper than the opposite south-facing slopes, where there are still meadows at the same altitude. The rowan and elder with their clusters of berries stand out in the mat of tall grasses which take advantage of the dampness of the soil enriched in nitrogen by the green alder. Wild garlic, alpine lettuce, masterwort and rosebay willowherb form dense clumps, whose shade favours the stitchwort, two-flowered pansy, round-leaved saxifrage and, on permanently damp rocks, the yellow mountain saxifrage.

The dunnock, garden warbler and lesser whitethroat, ring ousel and willow tit make their homes in the alder thickets. The black grouse or blackcock also hides away in their cover; he is only seen in spring when he emerges to perform his spectacular courtship displays on the open slopes above.

Above the upper limit of woodland, stunted by the browsing of cattle, a few isolated larches manage to survive in the sub-alpine moorland. The subsoil is still calcareous, as evidenced by the presence of blue moor grass, alpine daisy, fleabane and the large-flowered rockrose. The dwarf broom, of prostrate habit, is protected from the cold by the mantle of snow, and dwarf willows spread themselves out on the limestone rocks to make the most of the sun; the varieties reticulata, retusa and serpyllifolia are all to be found here.

Marsh marigolds, white bachelor's buttons and yellow mountain saxifrage flower along the stream, where the metallic notes of dippers and grey wagtails resound. Other birds, which nest in the cliff faces, patrol the sky over the sub-alpine moorland: alpine choughs with their yellow beaks, crag martins and the wallcreeper, a rare and striking species, whose rounded blackish wings have large red patches. Brown frogs inhabit the ponds and slow worms hide in the damp meadows, while the poisonous adder prefers the loose scree covered in vegetation.

### From Chalets de la Plagne to the Col du Palet

As the path climbs up a sill of gneiss, the Lac de la Plagne comes into view below. The lake is 18.5 metres deep, carved out of the gneiss by the great thickness of ice which accumulated behind the bar, or constriction. The lake has been half filled by the alluvial plain built up by the silt from mountain streams flowing into it. As we continue on up towards the Plan de la Grassaz, we cross some fine areas of sub-alpine grassland. On silicious terrain there is mountain arnica, alpine cinquefoil, cat's-foot and alpine bistort, while ragwort, and a variety of gentians - yellow, spotted, purple and bavarian - grow on the limestone.

The Aiguille de Bacque, 2,651 metres high, and the Aiguille des Aimes are limestone, whereas the Pointe du Chardonnet is part of the layer of glistening schists stretching from the Piedmont region, which the GR crosses after the Lac de Gratteleu. Higher still, gypsum and triassic dolomitic limestone show through on the Col du Palet at 2,652 metres. Continuing as far as the Col de la Croix des Frêtes, the striking north face of the Grande Casse comes into view, a sheer rock wall of limestone and schists more than 1,000 metres high. The peak itself, at 3,855 metres, is the highest in the Vanoise.

After the Plan de la Grassaz, at 2,320 metres, we have reached the true alpine level. The average annual temperature at this altitude is 0° C. Woody plants cannot survive at this level, apart from a few dwarf willows and dryas. The turf is noticeably thinner and new species make their appearance. On rocky, silicious areas we find alpine lovage, round-headed rampion and downy ragwort, and, on limestone, Hoppe's cudweed. Scree and rocks are the domain of purple saxifrage, stemless moss campion and 'chamois' cress. Beside the streams and ponds the starry saxifrage, glacial buttercup and snow gentian thrive. Finally, snow-covered combes are the refuge of least willow, alchemilla, alpine chrysanthemum, alpine speedwell and soldanella.

The rock pipit, wheatear, alpine accentor and snow finch inhabit the alpine turf, and you may be lucky enough to flush out a covey of ptarmigan among the rocks. The vast open landscape of the alpine level is the hunting ground of the golden eagle, while scavenging ravens keep the slopes clean.

From Rosuel onwards we would have heard marmots whistling. They are found right up to the alpine level, and so is the 'blue' hare which is white in winter, grey in summer! So too is the ermine or stoat, whose coat also changes colour with the seasons, except that the tip of its tail always remains black. If we stop for a breather near the rangers' observation chalet, we can see chamois and ibex which have come down to graze on the slopes of Mont Pourri and the Dôme des Platières.

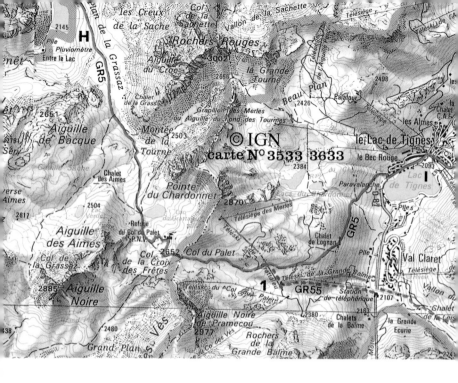

**Ruins of the former Chalet de la Grassaz**
*2,335m*

1:30

**REFUGE DU COL DU PALET**
⌂
*2,550m*
*There are many possible walks in the area: Tour de l'Aiguille Noire at 2,874 metres via the Col de la Croix des Frêtes, Lac du Grand Plan, Col de la Grassaz, Lac Verdet. From the Col de la Croix des Frêtes you can make your way back down to Champagny.*

0:15

**Col du Palet**
*2,652m*

Still walking in a southerly direction, climb the valley, keeping close to the stream. This brings you to the western end of the Lac du Grattaleu. A little further on, you reach the Refuge du Col du Palet.

Leaving the refuge, the GR continues upwards to the Col du Palet.

# A short glossary of mountain terms

| | |
|---|---|
| adret<br>endret | sunny, south facing mountain slope |
| avers<br>envers<br>ubac | north facing slope |
| balme<br>baume | cave |
| barre | sheer cliff |
| cairn | of Irish derivation (car=stone). A pile or heap of big or not so big stones, raised as a landmark or memorial; cairns may replace waymarks in some mountain areas |
| calm<br>cham | bare high plateau |
| claps<br>clapes<br>clapier | displaced boulders |
| cluse | gorge |
| combe | valley, generally dry |
| draille | track followed by herds of cattle during seasonal migrations (transhumance) |
| dranse | strong mountain stream (Alps) |
| étroit | gorge |
| estive<br>estibe | high altitude summer pasture |
| malpas | difficult section of pass |
| moraine | from the Savoyard word 'morena' (fold of earth): rock debris carried along by a glacier and deposited in various formations |
| pas | steep pass |
| peyre | isolated boulder marking the way |
| plagne<br>plan | small plain or plateau |
| praz | meadow |
| riou<br>riu<br>rec | small stream |
| serre | ridge between two hollows |
| thawaleg<br>talweg | thal=valley; weg=path: the steepest route up a valley; the line taken by running water (as in: 'walkers should follow the talweg') |

## La Haute Tarentaise

From the Col du Palet, the GR descends in an easterly direction, winding its way between swallow-holes where the gypsum has dissolved, until it comes to the Gratteleu ski lift, the first of a number of ski lifts.

**1:30**

**Junction** The GR55 leaves the GR5 on the right, to the southeast (see map ref I). Walkers who do not wish to go to Tignes-le-Lac can transfer to the GR55 and the 'High mountain' alternative route to Modane by following roughly the line of the Grande Balme ski lift down to the bridge over the Retort stream. Cross the stream and follow the line of a smaller ski lift until you come to a path, shortly before the Chalet de la Leisse, which is the continuation of the GR55 (see page 167).

The GR5 continues its descent, passing the Chalet de Lognan at 2,330 metres and joining the road into Tignes-le-Lac.

### TIGNES-LE-LAC
🏠 ⌂ ✕

*2,093m*
*(see map ref I)*

**0:30**

The GR5 passes behind the tennis courts and continues eastwards to the Pas de la Tovière.

### Pas de la Tovière
*2,252m*
*Views of Mont Blanc and Mont Pourri.*

**1:30**

The GR descends into the valley of the Tovière. At the Chalet de la Tovière at 2,118 metres, it crosses a stream and continues over the ski slopes. The path then broadens out, descends to the Val d'Isère electricity generating station and, passing the bridge over the river Isère on the left, skirts the southern edge of the resort.

The resort proper can be reached by crossing the bridge and turning right on the N202.

### VAL D'ISÈRE
🏠 ⌂ ✕ 🍷 �? 🚌 🅿

*1,809m*
*(see map ref J)*
*Ski and mountaineering resort.*

*On the following stage of the journey, you may be surprised to see signs to the*

At the cable-car station on the southern edge of Val d'Isère, double back towards the town for a short distance, then turn right, pass the chapelle Saint-Jean and continue straight on to Le Laisinant.

The GR follows the old Col d'Iseran road, unused since the N202 was opened. After the Floride chalet-hotel, turn left onto a path below Les Mélèzes chalet; cross the stream and leave

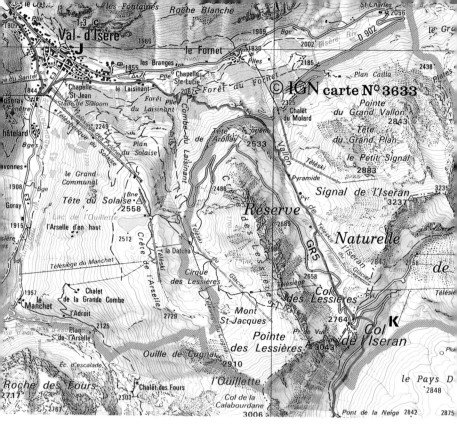

**3:30**

effect that you are entering a nature reserve, when in fact you are in the midst of a vast skiing area with an abundance of mechanical lifts. In this area plants and animals are protected, but there are no legal safeguards to prevent development of the site itself!

the path leading down to Le Fornet on your left. Climb up through woodland until you reach the N202; cross the road and continue on up the Iseran valley, keeping to the right bank of the stream. Further on, you will cross the stream and come to the N202 again. You cross the road twice more before reaching the Col de l'Iseran.

### Col de l'Iseran
*2,763m*
*(see map ref K)*

**0:40**

From the Col de l'Iseran (see map ref K), the GR5 makes its way downwards, shortcutting across a hairpin bend of the D902, which it rejoins for a few yards as far as a stone pyramid. The path then runs parallel with the road, joining it again shortly before the pont de la Neige.

## The Ptarmigan

A hundred or so different kinds of bird have been recorded in the National Park. One of the most typical species resident at high altitude is the ptarmigan.

In summer or winter plumage it blends in perfectly with its habitat. Not a shy bird, it can be seen scurrying tirelessly over scree and snow-covered ground.

## The Ermine or Stoat (Mustela erminea)

Brown in summer, entirely white in winter except for a tuft of black hair at the tip of its tail, the ermine has the same ability to change colour as the blue hare. Cruel, bloodthirsty hunters, agile and very inquisitive, ermine can be seen on the rocky slopes and nosing around chalets. Other mammals living in the Park include badgers in wooded areas, foxes up to quite high altitudes, weasels and snow voles.

## The Blue Hare

The blue hare is found in the highest alpine pastures, and will even take refuge on glaciers, should need arise.

Retiring, timid and preferring the hours of dusk or darkness for his activities, he is not easy to catch a glimpse of, especially as by successive moults, he changes from pure white in winter to grey-brown in summer, and is perfectly camouflaged on the rocky ground where he lies up.

Living only within the Arctic Circle and in high mountains elsewhere, the blue hare was left behind in the Alps when the quaternary glaciers retreated.

The hare is at home in most parts of the Park, and you are most likely to find his distinctive tracks in the snow.

The female gives birth in April and May to 2 or 3 leverets, about the size of a mouse, with a peculiar white splash on the forehead. The golden eagle takes a heavy toll of blue hares, his favourite prey after the marmot.

## La Haute-Maurienne

Though very close to La Tarentaise as the crow flies, the area you are now about to discover is very different in character - different in its physical structure, natural environment, history and people. On first acquaintance with this straight, dry valley, similar in some ways to the southern Alps, you may be affected by a feeling of harshness, or melancholy.

But gradually, step by step perhaps, like many others before you, you will come under the spell of this country, its ancient villages huddled around their church, its magnificent larch forests. Its people too, whose way of life may seem old-fashioned but who are endowed with special sensitivity, and an artistic sense rooted in the Baroque tradition of which this valley possesses the greatest French masterpieces.

Sensitivity and contemplation have been quite lost in urban civilisation, but here, perhaps better than anywhere else, you may discover them again in all their authenticity.

The GR5 is about to follow the valley of the Maurienne, on the edge of the National Park, at an average altitude of 2,000 metres. On this section of the walk you will have opportunity to enjoy mountain landscapes and to discover a rich wildlife protected in the Vanoise National Park. Before going further, please read the section of this book dealing with the Park and its rules.

If, on the other hand, you would prefer to explore old villages, wander from church to chapel, meet mountain people and their traditions, take the GR5E 'Sentier du Petit Bonheur' route, through the valley bottoms.

The following deals first with the GR5 Haute-Maurienne mountain route, and later with the GR5E Alternative Route, 'Villages de Haute-Maurienne', also known as the 'Sentier du Petit Bonheur'.

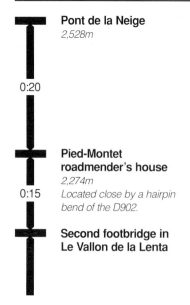

**Pont de la Neige**
*2,528m*

0:20

**Pied-Montet roadmender's house**
*2,274m*
*Located close by a hairpin bend of the D902.*

0:15

**Second footbridge in Le Vallon de la Lenta**

**Warning** Do not cross the bridge unless the path is badly snowed up; in this case it is important to take the D902.

Continue along the path until you come to the Ponts-et-Chaussées garage, cross the stream and go down into the gorge. Further on, recross the stream to reach the Pied-Montet roadmender's house.

Carry on down the left bank of the stream in the Lenta valley. Ignore the first footbridge and continue until you come to the second.

**Junction** The path leading to Bonneval-sur-Arc and the GR5E Alternative route 'Villages de Haute-Maurienne' leaves the GR5 (see page 179).

**Detour** *1 hr*
**BONNEVAL-SUR-ARC**
⌂ ⌂ ✕ 🅓
*1,783m*

2:15

**Detour** Do not cross the stream, but continue on the left bank. When you come to the road, turn south along it. A short distance further on, at the start of a hairpin bend in the road, turn off left on to a path which brings you down to Bonneval's electricity generating plant. Rejoin the GR5 by taking a path at the western end of the village; it cuts across 2 hairpin bends of the D902 and brings you out at Chalets des Roches at 2,400 metres (see map ref L).

The GR5 turns sharply to the west across the second footbridge in the Vallon de la Lenta

and follows the path to Les Druges as far as the Parc des Druges waymarker at 2,260 metres. Take the direction indicated - to the Refuge du Mollard. The GR5 re-enters the Vanoise National Park as the 'Sentier balcon de la Maurienne'. It winds to the edge of the Park at an altitude of 2,000 metres with views of the peaks forming the frontier with Italy rising up over the valley. When it crosses private property, the route of the GR5 is not always clearly marked; the path passes below the Pointe de la Met before coming to the Chalets des Roches.

**Chalets des Roches**
*2,453m*
*(see map ref L)*
*View of the Maurienne*
*peaks opposite.*

**Junction** The GR5 is rejoined by the path coming from Bonneval-sur-Arc.

1:15

From Chalets des Roches the GR5 brings you first to the Chalets de la Buffette and then, still on the 'Sentier balcon', to a very fine cirque with a waterfall descending from La Rocheure glacier, and a bridge over the Vallon stream at 2,240 metres. From here, the path leads downhill, passes an abandoned chalet and arrives at the Refuge du Mollard.

**REFUGE DU MOLLARD**
⌂

The GR now descends slightly to join the path to Le Villaron.

0:20

*2,230m*

**Path leading to Le Villaron**
*1,882m*

**Junction** The GR5E Alternative route from Le Villaron - indicated by a National Park sign - joins the GR5. The 2 GRs continue on the same route.

**Detour** *20 mins*
**LE VILLARON**
⌂ ✕

**Detour** Following the direction shown by the National Park sign take the GR5E path on the left.

*1,750m*

0:30

The GR5 continues down into the valley of the Arc with the opening of the Avérole valley opposite. It passes close to a cave dug into the cliff, then comes to a bridge leading to the village of Bessans.

**Junction** The GR5E separates from the GR5 at the bridge. (See map ref M). The GR5E crosses the river, goes through the village of Bessans and continues south along the left bank. The GR5 continues on the right bank of the Arc.

© IGN carte N° 36

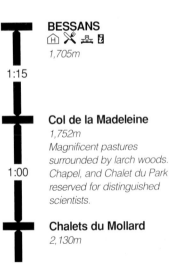

**BESSANS**

1,705m

1:15

**Col de la Madeleine**

1,752m
*Magnificent pastures
surrounded by larch woods.
Chapel, and Chalet du Park
reserved for distinguished
scientists.*

1:00

**Chalets du Mollard**

2,130m

The GR5 is a track with a stone kerb; it joins the D902 - at 1,675 metres - and follows the road in a westerly direction for a short way then turns right on to a path leading to the hamlet of Le Collet situated at the Col de la Madeleine.

To the right of the col, take the path signposted 'La Fesse-d'en-haut 2 h, Le Chatelard' which zigzags up steeply amid mediterranean vegetation to the Chalets du Mollard.

You will come to a fork, where a Park signpost indicates a detour to the Chalets du Chatelard, and where the GR5 itself turns west and follows

## Bessans

Bessans is not just any village. One distinguishing feature is its traditional costume - which you can see in a procession held on 15 August - with a headdress quite different from those of other communes in the Maurienne. But it also differs in its traditions, customs and history, all based on the simple faith of country people, and a very special faith at that: as they sing in their old Christmas carols, Jesus was born at Bessans, not Bethlehem!

Some of the people of Bessans have always had to emigrate, since the village could not support them all. After Savoy was joined to France in 1860, Paris became the usual goal of seasonal migrations, particularly the Levallois-Perret district, where many Bessannais are now taxi drivers.

Here perhaps more than in other places, man is subject to the vagaries of nature. Bessans surrounded by slopes that are prone to avalanches and, though all precautionary measures are taken, the threat remains. In such circumstances, man's last resort is to what he holds sacred, and to prayer.

This may explain the proliferation of chapels and oratories in this area. Make a point of visiting the Chapelle Saint-Antoine, next to the church (for access, ask at the presbytery).

On the outer wall of this chapel are frescoes depicting a cavalcade of the vices, chained together and drawn along to hell by two devils. They are followed by the virtues, a favourite theme of 17th century mural painters in the Western Alps. Inside, a series of forty scenes portrays the life of Christ; the artist is unknown, but the date of 1526, on one of the roof beams probably relates to their completion. Statues, carved figures in brightly-painted wood and painted panels from other chapels in the neighbourhood have been brought together in this building to protect them against the dangers of theft and vandalism. Bessans' glorious artistic traditions, especially the school of sculpture associated with the Clappier family in the 16th century, are continued today in local craftmanship (devils, hens ...). Some examples are on show at the Syndicat d'initiative.

---

**1:00**

**La Fesse-d'en-haut**
*2,290m*
*Inhabited in summer; cross and chapel.*

**REFUGE DU VALLONBRUN**
⌂ ✗
*2,272m*

**Detour** *2 hrs*
*La Pierre-aux-Pieds*

the border of the Park to the hamlet of La Fesse-d'en-haut.

The GR continues to the Refuge du Vallonbrun.

The GR5 continues westward, passes the hamlet of La Fesse-du-Milieu, cuts across a valley at 2,330 metres, then another smaller one, and soon after comes to a path leading to 'La Pierre aux Pieds'.

The path then crosses a series of combes, passing chalets at Le Coin Haut and Les Essarts, to the Chalet du Coin Bas.

**La Pierre-aux-Pieds**

The stone is a huge block of polished schist, with 50 or so small carved feet facing east. Its origins and the reasons for these feet are still a mystery to archaeologists. Perhaps it dates from the neolithic period, perhaps it was a sacrificial altar, the blood collecting in the hollows of the rock, an initiation rite for children who had reached puberty? Resist the temptation to climb up on to the rock without taking your shoes off: this stone has become quite severely worn in the few years since it became known to walkers, and its markings, which may date back 7,000 years, could be lost in the next 10 or 15. The damage is caused by the soles of walking boots.

**Chalet du Coin Bas**
*2,040m*

**Detour** *1 hr*
**LANSLEVILLARD**
Ⓗ ✕ 🚉 🅱
*1,500m*

1:45

**Ruins of Pramaria**
*2,100m*

**Detour** *1 hr*
**LANSLEBOURG-MONT-CENIS**
Ⓗ ✕ 🚉 🅱
*1,400m*
additional *1 hr 30 minutes to*
**TERMIGNON**
Ⓗ ◯ ⋀ ✕ 🚉 🅱
*1,300m*

**REFUGE DU CUCHET**
◯
*2,160m*

2:30

**Detour** From the Chalet du Coin Bas take the path descending down to the left.

The GR next crosses the combes of the Nay and Plâtre streams and, shortly before the Cugnet, comes to the ruins of Pramaria.

**Detour** From the ruins take the path on the left leading down to Lanslebourg-Mont-Cenis. To continue to Termignon, cross the river Arc by the bridges from the N6 road, which runs through the village, and turn immediately right on to the GR5E Alternative Route coming from Lanslevillard. The GR5E runs along the river bank opposite the village and continues westward through the Forêt d'Arc to Termignon. The GR5 can be regained by a second path climbing north-west from the reservoir at Lanslebourg and reaching the GR to the west of the ruins of Pramaria, at Pré Vaillant.

A little further on from Pramaria, the GR5 reaches the Refuge du Cuchet.

The GR carries on westward, passing the ruins of Rochasses, and eventually comes to a crossroads at the Chalets of Pré Vailland, where the alternative path from Lanslebourg-Mont-Cenis comes in on the left. The GR turns north and leads uphill to the Chalets de la Turra de Termignon.

## Chalets de la Turra de Termignon

*2,290m*

*Chalets built on the south-western spur of the La Crête de la Turra as it descends from La Pointe du Grand-Vallon.*

2:15

From the Chalets de la Turra de Termignon, the GR5 describes a huge loop outside the National Park keeping at an almost constant altitude. After passing chalets at Bercheren and at La Fema, it enters the Park again. The path then leads north east to the Bellecombe car park (see map ref O) at the junction of the road coming up from Termignon. There is a road which goes on to Entre-deux-Eaux via La Porte du Parc du Plan du Lac, but you can avoid it by taking a path leading off on the right, above the Bellecombe car park. This path brings you to La Porte du Parc du Plan du Lac.

## LA PORTE DU PARC DU PLAN DU LAC
⌂ ✕

*2,364m*

*Fine view of the Vanoise chain of glaciers to the west, and the Park's highest peaks to the north: La Grande Casse and La Grande Motte, half hidden by the limestone cliffs of Pierre Brune. Going west from the refuge, you can reach the top of the Doron de Termignon gorges, a common haunt of alpine ibex. On the opposite side of the valley, in the moraines of the Pelve glacier, chamois are abundant.*

0:30

From the Porte du Parc du Plan du Lac, the GR5 goes along the road closed to tourist traffic as far as the Chapelle Saint-Bartélémy; there, take a path on the left which descends to La Rocheure stream but does not cross it.

## La Rocheure stream

*2,053m*

*(see map ref P)*

**Detour** *20 mins*

## REFUGE D'ENTRE-DEUX-EAUX
⌂ ✕

*2,120m*

**Detour** Cross La Rocheure stream and climb up the other side until you come to the refuge.

From the refuge, a 20 minute walk will bring you to the GR55 at Pont de Cro-Vie - 2,099 metres. If you cross the bridge, the path takes you to the Refuge de la Vanoise and on to Pralognan. In the other direction, the GR55 leads back to Tignes, via the valley and the Col de la Liesse.

### The Alpine Ibex

Huge annulated horns almost a metre in length, one hundred kilos of steely muscle under a coat which blends in perfectly with the rocks of its mountain fastnesses: such is the adult male Alpine ibex.

Sturdy-looking, rather lazy and apathetic in temperament, its feet firmly planted on a grassy ledge on one of the spectacular vertical rock faces which it frequents, this magnificent Alpine beast seems to care nothing for the passage of time, numbing cold, heights or even the presence of man.

It rarely leaves these high altitudes, feeding early in the morning and late in the evening, and choosing a cool spot higher up to ruminate during the hotter part of the day.

At the first snowfall, the males rejoin the smaller, more timid, females which, with their shorter horns, are more like their distant cousin the domestic goat. During this season, the mountains ring with the clash of the males' horns, as they challenge one another to repeated, but never fatal, trials of strength.

The females give birth in late June and early July and, in a matter of days, the kids are able to follow their mothers on to the steepest crags.

The main herds are to be seen in the Poiset, Arpont, Grande Casse and Mont Pourri massifs.

## The Marmot

Friendly little creatures, a typical mountain people, whose very presence adds a touch of eccentric, good-natured humour to the rather harsh landscape. It is they, of course, who have given rise to all the old stories of gnomes, 'little people', and guardians of buried treasure so common in the myths of northern lands. And one has to admit that, bundled up in their thick fur coats, with their guileless expression, comical stance, prehensile 'hands' and habit of standing on their back legs to nibble at some particularly juicy blade of grass, have a good look round or sound the alarm, it is difficult not to think of them as endearing little simpletons.

Dawn is the time to watch them, as soon as the sun starts to warm up the threshold of their burrows. Then, with infinite precaution, they stick the tips of their noses outside, take a step forward, then a step back, spend minutes scrutinizing the familiar landscape, as if it had conspired to become hostile territory during the hours of darkness! At last, satisfied that no one is about and the world is at peace, their stomachs crying out for sustenance, they make up their minds to hop out and enjoy the traditional marmot breakfast.

This is the hour of their longest sorties, which may take them as much as 100 metres from the safety of home. But at the mere movement of a shadow on the moraine, a stone slipping on the snowfield, or a crow that squawks as it dives, and the little cowards dash back to their holes like a set of jack-in-the-boxes, and breakfast will have to wait until they have been through the whole ritual again.

**Samivel** *Peaks and Wonders (Artaud)*

Detour
**Memorial to the Alpine Regiments**

4:00

The GR5 follows the left bank of the Rocheure stream and eventually crosses it via a footbridge. It then turns left and crosses a second footbridge over the Liesse stream before leading on to the Chalets d l'Ile. Here it zigzags up the very steep slopes of Mont de la Para.

**Detour** As you climb, take, on your right, a Park path at 2,329 metres which follows the eastern flank of the plateau of La Réchasse before joining the GR55 near the monument erected in memory of the alpine regiments.

The GR5 makes a hairpin bend south west to the left and continues to climb. On one of the last hairpins, on the left, about ten metres from the path, you will see an enormous table of stone. This is one of many 'acorn-cup' stones found in the Haute-Maurienne, and may have been dug out in the neolithic period. The GR now passes several small lakes surrounded by smooth rocks polished by the Pelve glacier, then comes to a huge moraine. Above this moraine lie the Ferran lakes, one of the most beautiful sights in the Vanoise National Park. After the Moraine des Lacs Ferran, the path crosses the Pelve plateau, then runs parallel with the gorges of the Doron de Termignon where you may catch an occasional glimpse of alpine ibex.

**Warning** This part of the route, especially near the Refuge de l'Arpont, may be dangerous if the ground is still icy. Proceed with care. You are unlikely to encounter ice patches after the beginning of July.

The next landmark is the Refuge de l'Arpont.

## REFUGE DE L'ARPONT

⌂ ✕

*2,309m*
*Marmots and ibex in the vicinity.*

The GR5 passes a cattle pen at the Chalets de l'Arpont, then the Chapelle Saint-Laurent, and continues, keeping to the side of the valley, towards the Chalets du Mont.

## Chalets du Mont
*2,095m*

**Detour** *1 hr 30 mins*
## TERMIGNON
🏠 ⌂ Å ✕ ⚒ 🅱
*1,300m*

**1:00**

**Detour** Close by the Chalets du Mont, a path on the left leaves the GR, indicated by a Park sign. The path passes the Chalets de l'Esseillon before reaching the D83 road at Pont du Chatelard. It follows the road into Termignon.

The GR5 climbs the Combe d'Enfer on the left bank of the Grand Pyx stream as it descends from the Mahure glacier, then crosses the stream via a small bridge. The path zigzags through 2 hairpin bends to negotiate a rise, before leading down to the Chalets de Montafia.

## Chalets de Montafia
*2,152m*

**Detour** *1 hr 30 mins*
**Termignon**
*1,300m*

1:20

**Detour** *2 hrs*
**Sollières**
*1,300m*

**Chalets de la Loza**
*2,327m*
*Roofs of the chalets are covered in orangy-red lichen; from the Cross, a fine view of La Dent Parrachée, La Grande Motte and La Grande Casse.*

1:45

**Detour** *1 hr 30 mins*
**Sardières**
*1,498m*

**Ruins of the Chalets de la Turra**
*2,360m*
**Detour**
**Monolith de Sardières**

**Detour** See page 157 for details of accommodation etc. A path branching off to the left (see map ref G), near the Chalets de Montafia willl bring you down to Termignon.

The GR5 traverses an almost local course - 2,150 to 2,220 metres - a combe abutting upon the Chalets de la Ferrière. A series of hairpin bends brings you up through the meadows to the foot of the easternmost pillar of La Dent Parrachée at an altitude of about 2,400 metres. The path levels out and runs first through meadows, then among large boulders and finally over scree, until you come to the foot of La Dent Parrachée itself, in a wild, high mountain landscape. Continue along the mountain side and cross a combe scored by the Bonne Nuit stream.

**Detour** Follow the Bonne Nuit stream on its bank valleywards to Sollières on the GR5E Haute-Maurienne Villages Alternative Route.

The GR5 continues past a spring before climbing to a shelf on which the Chalets de la Loza are situated.

**Detour** From the Chalets de la Loza a path on the left leads down to the village of Sardières.

From the Chalets de la Loza, the GR5 follows the military road which leads gently down to the foot of the Roc des Corneilles, then by broad hairpin bends to the ruins of the Chalets de la Turra.

**Detour** At the chalet ruins a path to the left leading down into the valley brings you to the monolith and on to the village of Sardières.

The GR5 continues in a south-westerly direction towards the lakes of Plan d'Aval and Plan d'Amont.

**Detour** *30 mins*
**REFUGE DE PLAN SEC**
⌂ ✕ ⍾

**Detour** Shortly before Le Djoin chair lift a path branches off to the right which leads to the Refuge de Plan Sec.

The GR continues to a place known as le Djoin and there turns north to circumvent the 2 lakes. It passes first the Chalet de la Randolière, and then the Chalet de la Fournache.

**Chalet de la Fournache**
*2,330m*

**Detour**
**REFUGE DE LA DENT PARRACHÉE**
⌂

**Detour** At the Chalet de la Fournache a path branches off northwards to the Refuge de la Dent Parrachée.

3:00

The GR5 then turns westwards and comes to the junction of another path.

**Detour**
**REFUGE DU FOND D'AUSSOIS**
⌂
*2,324m*

**Detour** At the junction a path leaves the GR on the right and leads northwards to the Refuge du Fond d'Aussois.

The GR path leads down and across a stream at 2,206 metres then begins climbing again in a south-westerly direction; after reaching a plateau at 2,245 metres it turns south eastwards. From here, you have a bird's eye view of the 2 lakes, the Plan d'Amont and the Plan d'Aval. The GR then turns due south.

**Detour**
**AUSSOIS**
⌂ ✕
*1,483m*

**Detour** The GR comes to a path on the left leading steeply down to the dam at the foot of the Plan d'Aval. From the dam the route follows the road down to the south east, past a chapel, and short cuts wide hairpin bends to Aussois. At Aussois it meets the extension of the GR5E from Bramans.

The GR continues south to the Col du Barbier.

**Col du Barbier**
*2,287m*

After a gentle climb to the Chalets du Barbier, the GR pursues a more or less level course to the west. You pass a spring, 10 metres above the pathway, as you cross the combe leading down to the village of Le Bourget. Going through

1:30

**Chalets de l'Orgère**
*1,895m*
*(see map ref S)*

0:20

**PORTE DU PARC DE L'ORGÈRE**

*1,935m*
*Refuge belonging to the Vanoise National Park.*

0:30 | **Detour** *2 hrs*
**Lac de la Partie**
*2,458m*

Le Bourget forest of stone pines, the path first leads downwards then climbs again to the Chalets de l'Orgère.

The path turns north and crosses the meadows of the Orgère valley, after crossing a stream, it passes a chapel and reaches the D106 road which it follows, turning right, to the Porte du Parc de l'Orgère.

**Detour** From above the refuge take a park trail northwards, joining the GR55 - which crosses the National Park from north to south - to the Lac de la Partie.

From Refuge de l'Orgère, the GR descends in a south-westerly direction, rejoining and following the D106 westwards as far as the bridge over the Saint Bernard stream.

Vanoise. L'Orgère

## The Chamois

The chamois is widespread throughout the Vanoise National Park and has never been in danger of extinction in this region. There were about 400 head when the park was established, rising to 4,000 by the 1979 census, an average annual rate of increase of 17%.

Unlike the ibex, the chamois is not a member of the goat family, but more closely related to the antelopes. There is little danger of confusing the two species, as they differ considerably in size - an adult chamois weighs 30 to 40 kilogrammes - and in the shape and length of their horns: the chamois' are slender and hook sharply backwards at the ends. The chamois is also slimmer in outline and much quicker in making its getaway than the ibex.

Not a sun-seeker, the chamois shows a preference for shady combes and the cooler slopes, and is quite at home in the snow and on icefields, to which its hard sharp hooves are well adapted.

Males and females look very similar in autumn, when their coat takes on a darker hue. This is the rutting season, when the males engage in fierce combat and pursue one another relentlessly. The young are born the following May when they and their mothers congregate in large herds, often more than 200 strong. The young chamois are endowed with remarkable vitality, which they display in playful antics, racing about and sliding on the névés.

**Saint Bernard Stream**
*1,770m*

0:30

**Chalets de la Perrière**
*1,670m*

1:00

**Loutraz**
*1,064m*
0:10  *Suburb of Modane.*

**MODANE**
🏠 ⌂ ✕ ⏛ ⛓ 🚌 🚃 🛈
*1,066m*
*An industrial town on the N6
with an international
atmosphere, being close to
the Italian border; it was a
defensive stronghold of first
importance, a fact attested
to by the many forts around
the town; Modane lies in the
heart of La Maurienne, in
the beautiful Arc valley,
overlooked to the south by
a forested ridge, to the
north and north east by the
Chasseforêt massif and to
the north west by the
Péclet-Polset massif; it
suffered badly in the 1939-
45 war and has been
damaged more recently by
the flooding of the Arc.*

**Junction** The GR5 joins the GR55 coming from the Col de Chavière and the hamlet of Polset.

Continuing southwards, the GR5 and the GR55 follow the same route along a bridle path on the right bank of the stream to the Chalets de la Perrière and beyond to Modane.

The track leaves the stream and zizags down through several hairpin bends towards meadows above the town of Modane. Crossing steep areas of scree, it reaches Loutraz.

Cross the river Arc and you are in the heart of Modane.

The GR5 continues on southwards to the Hautes-Alpes; crossing the Briançonnais and the Queyras regions, it reaches the Ubaye valley.

# GR55

## 'High mountain' Alternative Route

The GR55 crosses the Vanoise National Park from north to south, following a route at higher altitudes than the GR5, so giving it the name of 'High mountain' Alternative route. In fact, apart from Pralognan where it descends to 1,500 metres, it remains constantly at altitudes of between 2,000 and 2,600 metres. Along the way, it crosses the Col de la Chavière, at 2,796 metres the highest pass crossed by any GR.

The route can be walked in 4 days. Accommodation is in refuges, except at Pralognan where there are hotels.

Walkers may still find unmelted icefields persisting quite late into the season at the Col de la Leisse at 2,758 metres and the Col de la Chavière at 2,796 metres.

With luck and plenty of patience, you will be able to observe ibex and chamois, while marmots will give warning of your approach with piercing whistles. With its wild scenery and magnificent views, the GR55 offers all the splendour of a high mountain region.

The GR55 starts from its junction with the GR5 (see map ref 1), south west of the Lac de Tignes, by the ski lifts of the resort of Val Claret.

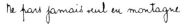

Vanoise, Les Evettes

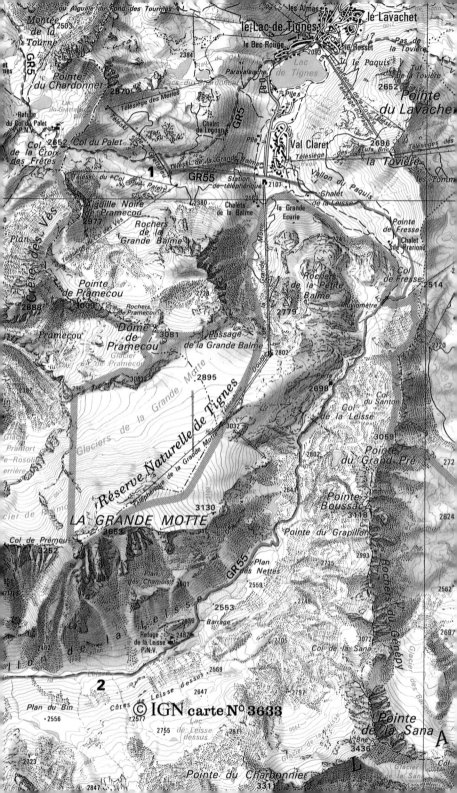

## VAL-CLARET
⌂ ✕

*2,100m*

*There is a big contrast between the 2 sides of the valley. The right-hand side consists of softer rocks: gypsums, dolomitic limestone and tuff, which form fairly gentle slopes suitable for skiing. Opposite are the steep limestone cliffs of the Petite-Balme.*

1:40

Follow a path leading up to the Chalet de la Liesse, then climb the Paquis valley to a number of small lakes.

After passing above the Chalet de Prariond, you come to the junction at the Col de Fresse.

## Col de Fresse junction
*2,531m*

Leave the path up to the Col de Fresse, at 2,576 metres, on your left and carry on south-south-westwards. The path climbs among rocks in a wild landscape between the Grande-Motte massif and the summit of Le Grande-Pré. **Warning** Take care not to miss the cairns - small piles of rock - which mark the way at some points, up to and beyond the Col de Leisse.

1:15

## Col de la Leisse
*2,758m*
*Dominated by the Grande-Motte glacier; icefields persist here until late in the season; to the north you will see the high, ravined cliffs of glistening schists of Grande-Sassière.*

The GR55 leads downwards into an area of scree. Look out for the cairns; the path is not easy to follow. You will pass the eastern shore of Lac Nettes and come to its southern end. The path becomes clearer again as you cross the Plan des Nettes, an area of alpine pasture, where you may hear marmots whistling. Follow the right bank of the stream. Shortly after a small dam, you come to the Refuge de la Leisse.

## REFUGE DE LA LEISSE
⌂

*2,487m*
*Marmots abound in the Leisse valley (see map ref 2); ibex and chamois may be glimpsed on the rocky slopes below La Grande-Casse.*

1:30

Soon after leaving the Refuge de la Leisse, the GR crosses over to the left bank of La Leisse stream.

The path follows the Leisse downwards as far as a stone bridge, the Pont de Croé-Vie.

## Pont de Croé-vie
*2,099m*
**Detour** *20 mins*
## REFUGE D'ENTRE-DEUX-EAUX

**Detour** Do not cross the bridge, but follow the path on the left bank southwards to the refuge. It is possible to rejoin the GR5 by continuing

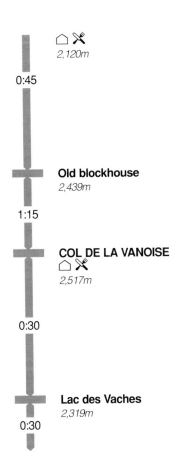

⌂ ✕
*2,120m*

0:45

**Old blockhouse**
*2,439m*

1:15

**COL DE LA VANOISE**
⌂ ✕
*2,517m*

0:30

**Lac des Vaches**
*2,319m*

0:30

further south to the bridge over La Rocheure stream.

The GR55 crosses the Leisse by the Pont de Croé-Vie and zigzags sharply in hairpin bends up the side of the Réchasse mountain. You will pass a monument to 2 officers of the alpine regiment, who died in the mountains. The next landmark is an old blockhouse.

The GR55 turns westward, breasts a rise, runs parallel with La Vanoise stream for a while, then crosses the stream at about 2,445 metres. Passing Le Lac Rond, the path brings you to the Col de la Vanoise.

From the Col de la Vanoise to Pralognan, the GR55 follows the ancient glacial valley of La Grande-Casse, which is constricted by steepsided spurs.

From the Refuge du Col de la Vanoise, the GR55 follows a mule track running parallel with the west bank of Le Lac Long, and then by hairpin bends across an area of scree it reaches Le Lac des Vaches.

Ford the lake on the large stepping stones. Further on, cross a stream at 2,210 metres and leave the Vanoise National Park shortly before coming to the Chalets de la Glière.

©IGN
carte N° 3533
Pointe du Vallonnet
Pointe des Volnets
Pointe du Creux Noir
Pointe de Leschaux
Aiguille du Bochor
Aiguille de la Vanoise
Col de la Vanoise
Refuge du Col de la Vanoise (Félix Faure) (C.A.F.)
Refuge du Grand Bec (C.A.F.)
Chalet des Gardes
Chalets de la Glière
Mont Bochor
Mont Chevrier
le Moriond
Grande Aiguille de l'Arcelin
le Grand Marchet
le Petit Marchet
Pointe du Dard
Roche Ferran
Rochers du Génépy
Pralognan-la-Vanoise
les Granges
les Darbelays
les Fontanettes
le Barioz
Bois de la Glière
Bois du Creuset
Forêt d'Isertan
Bois de la Rossa
Aiguille d'Août
Aig. de Mey
Rocher de Plassa
Dents de la Portetta
Crête du Mont Charvet
la Croix
la Novaz
Bonneval
du Villard
GR55
D 915
3
4

## Chalets de la Glière
*2,030m*

**0:40**

## Les Fontanettes
*1,664m*

**0:20**

## PRALOGNAN-LA-VANOISE
🏠 ⌂ Å ✗ ⛾ ⚒ ₿
*1,418m*
*A skiing and mountaineering centre.*

**0:45**

## Pont de Gerlon
*1,592m*
*Between the Gerlon and La Pêche bridges, the path runs through meadows rich in wild flowers and oat grass, some still being cut for hay.*

**0:45**

## Pont de la Péche
*1,764m*
*Some 30 or 40 metres above the bridge, a bank of water-loving willows and small birches cuts across the path - the last trees to border the footpath. The meadows here are not cut for hay, so you can enjoy the large yellow gentian and knapweed in bloom.*

## Detour *7 hrs*
## La Maurienne
*Detour This Park path crosses over the Col d'Aussois up to 2,916 metres and into La Maurienne. The route over the pass is quite difficult - grade 3.*
*In the meadows among the rocks, are bushes of*

**2:30**

Continue over the area of level ground and cross La Glière stream at 2,010 metres. The path now enters a forest and runs parallel with the cables of a ski lift down to the hamlet of Les Fontanettes.

The GR55 continues on down, shortcutting the hairpin bends in the road. Itpasses through the hamlets of Les Bieux and Le Barioz to arrive at Pralognan-la-Vanoise.

The GR55 leaves the village at the south end, following a road to the camp site which brings you to the edge of the Isertan forest. From here, follow the right bank of the Chavière as far as the Pont de Gerlon.

The GR55 crosses the Pont de Gerlon to the left bank and follows a track to the hamlet of Les Prioux; there it crosses the stream again and joins the road for 2 kilometres as far as the Pont de la Pêche.

Cross over to the left bank again and climb up through the alpine meadows following the Doron de Chavière valley.

A little further on, you pass a path leading off on the right to the Col du Mône and the foot of Le Petit Mont Blanc. The route then takes you past the chalets at La Motte and Chapendu to the Ritort oratory, where another path leads off, on the left, to the Col d'Aussois.

From the Ritort signpost, you can see some large cowsheds on the right bank of the Doron de Chavière, with several hectares of mountain sorrel in the foreground.

The GR55 continues its gradual climb up the Doron de Valprement valley.Passing chalets at Le Mollaret d'en Bas and La Rama, it comes to the Refuge de Péclet-Polset situated a little way off to the right of the GR.

*mezereon, whose flowers push up through the snow in spring before the leaves are formed.*

### REFUGE DE PÉCLET-POLSET
⌂ ✕

*2,474m*

**Detour** *20 mins*
**Le Lac Blanc**

*2,429m*

*Detour From the Refuge de Péclet-Polset, climb the slope to the northwest.*

1:15

*Among the rivulets feeding this lake some splendid glacial ranunculus are to be found, with colours ranging from red to white.*

The track to the Refuge de Péclet-Polset allows you to get back onto the GR without retracing your steps. The path now climbs steadily and brings you to areas of compacted snow, which may persist well into the season. Crossing these névés, you arrive at the Col de Chavière.

### Col de Chavière

*2,796m*

*The highest pass crossed by any GR; on a clear day you can see the principal glaciers in the Vanoise, and the peaks of Mont Blanc, Le Pelvoux, Les Écrins, Le Thabor and Le Viso.*

0:45

The GR55 descends over scree - be careful to follow the cairns - and comes to a rocky cirque with the Lac de la Partie. You reach a kind of plateau, at the end of which, at 2,504 metres, 2 paths meet.

### Fork

*2,504m*

**Detour** *2 hrs 15 mins*
### REFUGE AND PORTE DU PARC DE L'ORGÈRE
⌂ ✕

*1,935m*

*This route will be of special interest to lovers of alpine wildlife. You can see any number of marmots, given a degree of luck and plenty of patience, chamois below the Rteau d'Aussois, and ibex in the Aiguille Doran area. You may be lucky*

1:30

**Detour** Take the fork to the left. A National Park path, it will take you without difficulty to the refuge and the Porte du Parc. From there the D106 road leads down to Saint-André in the suburbs of Modane.

The GR55 takes the right-hand fork and leads steeply downhill, crossing the area known as Le Grand Planay.

The path now goes through woodland and descends the left bank of the Saint-Bernard stream to the hamlet of Polset.

*enough to see ibex in the rocky ridges to the east of the path.*

**Polset**
*1,840m*

The GR follows a track leading to the bridge where the D106 road crosses the Saint-Bernard stream.

**Junction** The GR55 joins the GR5 coming from the Porte du Parc de l'Orgère.

**0:30**

The GR55 and GR5 continuing southwards now follow the same route along a bridle path on the right bank of the stream to the Chalets de la Perrière and beyond to Modane.

**Chalets de la Perrière**
*1,670m*

The track leaves the stream and zigzags down through several hairpin bends towards meadows above the town of Modane. Crossing steep areas of scree, it reaches Loutraz.

**1:00**

**Loutraz**
*1,064m*
*Suburb of Modane*

Cross the river Arc and you are in the heart of Modane.

**0:10**

**MODANE**
🏠 ⌂ ✕ ⍭ ⛓ 🚐 🚆 🅿

*1,066m*
*An industrial town on the N6 with an international atmosphere, being close to the Italian border; it was a defensive stronghold of first importance, a fact attested to by the many forts around the town; Modane lies in the heart of La Maurienne, in the beautiful Arc valley, overlooked to the south by a forested ridge, to the north and north east by the Chasse forêt Massive, and to the north west by the Péclet-Polset massif; it suffered badly in the 1939-45 war and has been damaged more recently by the flooding of the Arc.*

# GR5E

## 'Haute-Maurienne Villages' Alternative Route 'Sentier du Petit Bonheur'

The GR5E 'Haute-Maurienne Villages' Alternative Route 'Sentier du Petit Bonheur' - from Bonneval-sur-Arc to Bramans (see pages 142 to 145). Walkers coming from the GR5 - Val d'Isère (see map ref J) - Col de l'Iseran (see map ref K; 3 hrs 30 mins) - Pied-Montet roadmender's house (60 mins) - join the GR5E by a path from the second footbridge in the Lenta valley, a 15 minutes' walk from the roadmender's house, and 1 hour's walk to Bonneval. Do not cross the stream, but continue on the left bank to the D902 road from Val d'Isère. Turn south along the road and a short distance farther on, at the start of the first hairpin bend, turn left on to a path which goes down to the electricity generating plant at Bonneval-sur-Arc.

### BONNEVAL-SUR-ARC
🏠 ⌂ ✕ 🛈

*1,783m*
*Typical village of La Haute-Maurienne, and unique in having maintained its original character; take time to stroll in its unspoilt streets.*

1:30

*The hamlet of Écot, up the valley to the east, is well worth a special visit. Until recently it was, at 2,000 metres, the highest inhabited village in France. A few houses are still occupied in summer, but in winter the stone chalets roofed with shingles are deserted and silent.*

The GR5E or 'Sentier du Petit Bonheur' leaves the village at its western end, passes an oratory and follows the right bank of the Arc. You will pass the hamlet of l'Évasset and, shortly after, cross the Vallon stream. You are dominated by the 'Rocher du Château' at this point. A few years ago, rock paintings representing deer were discovered on this huge block of serpentine. The path leads through a larch forest before coming to the hamlet of Villaron.

The red and white waymarks are often few and far between and at times non-existent, but walkers will find satisfaction in working out their route with the aid of a map. Waymarking should be seen as a support, to reassure walkers and help them learn the ropes. With experience, they should be able to find their way using just a map, a compass, and a smattering of place names and landmarks.

Pas de raccourcis inconnus.

## VILLARON
⌂ ✗

*1,750m*
*Characteristic local building*
*style; chapel with a cross*
*displaying the symbols of*
*the Passion; note carved*
*beam on the third house*
*after chapel.*

## BESSANS
⌂ ✗ ⚒ 🛈

*1,705m*
*(see map ref M)*
*A good starting point for*
*any number of excursions*
*into the Avérole and Ribon*
*valleys. In the Avérole valley*
*there is a CAF refuge.*

2:30

**Detour**
**La Pierre des Saints**

## LANSLEVILLARD
⌂ ✗ ⚒ 🛈

*1,500m*
*Above the church, behind*
*the mairie, is the chapel of*
*Saint-Sébastien; apply at*
*the presbytery for*
*permission; the walls of the*
*nave are painted with*
*frescoes; on the eastern*
*part of the south wall are 17*
*scenes from the life of Saint*
*Sebastien, while those*
*beginning on the western*
*part depict the life of Christ.*

0:30

## LANSLEBOURG-
## MONT-CENIS
⌂ ✗ ⚒ 🛈

*1,400m*
*You will be surprised to find*
*two church buildings facing*

**Junction** The GR5E climbs up through the village and joins the GR5. The 2 GRs continue on the same route as far as the bridge at Bessans. The GR5 continues on the right bank of the Arc. The GR5E crosses the bridge into the village.

At the western end of the village, the GR5E follows a minor road on the left bank of the river. It crosses the Ribon over the Charriondaz bridge and comes out on to the D902 road near a camp site. Cross the road and continue through woodland along the river to the Chalets of Chantelouve d'en Bas.

**Detour** From the Chalets of Chantelouve d'en Bas take the path on the left of the GR climbing up to La Pierre des Saints, an impressive 'acorn cup' stone.

Emerging from the woods, you will see the village of Lanslevillard .

Keep to the left bank of the Arc until you reach the village of Lanslebourg-Mont-Cenis, reached by crossing one of the bridges.

If you did not cross the Arc to visit Lanslebourg, continue on the left bank of the river. After walking through the Arc forest, you will come to Termignon.

**1:30**

*one another; the older church structure, to the north, was built in 1677, consisting of 3 naves; the bell tower was rebuilt in 1761; later the 2 outer naves were destroyed; served at various times as mairie, court house and school, and now the 'Centre d'Animation de la Vanoise' [Vanoise cultural activities centre].*

### TERMIGNON
⌂ ◠ 🅰 ✖ 🚉 🄴

*1,300m*
*This old village has some interesting features; its church, largely rebuilt in the 17th century is one of the baroque churches for which La Haute-Maurienne is famous; with some fine screens; the altar of the rosary on the right probably the work of Jean Clappier (1626).*

**0:30**

The GR5E leaves Termignon, continues southwards, keeping to the left bank of the Arc to Sollières.

### Sollières
*1,300m*
*There are really 2 villages here: Sollières l'Envers and Sollières l'Adroit, north and south-facing; Sollières l'Envers has an exhibition hall devoted to archaeology.*

**1:30**

Via the hamlets of l'Envers, Le Chatelet and Le Verney, the GR5E leads to Bramans.

### BRAMANS
◠ ✖

*1,250m*
*Not far from here, in the direction of Ambin valley, is Saint-Pierre- d'Extravache, the last church of interest on this 'Sentier du Petit Bonheur' route.*

The GR5E continues from Braman, through Aussois, and rejoins the GR5 just beyond Plan d'Aval.

# ACCOMMODATION GUIDE

The many different kinds of accommodation in France are explained in the introduction. Here we include a selection of hotels and other addresses, which is by no means exhaustive – the hotels listed are usually in the one-star or two-star categories. We have given full postal addresses where available so bookings can be made.

There has been an explosive growth in bed and breakfast facilities (chambres d'hôte) in the past few years, and staying in these private homes can be especially interesting and rewarding. Local shops and the town hall (mairie) can usually direct you to one.

**Ambin**
73300 Saint Jean de
Maurienne
⌂ d'Ambin
☎ 79.64.35.31
⌂ des Glaciers
☎ 79.05.22.32
or 79.05.08.73

**Antème**
⌂
☎ 25.79.13.40

**Anterne**
⌂ Alfred Wills
☎ 50.34.91.63
⌂ Moède
☎ 50.53.43.23
or 50.53.46.99

**Arpont**
⌂ de l'Arpont
Mme Charon
☎ 79.20.51.51
or 79.62.30.54

**Averole**
⌂ d'Averole
Mr Josseron
☎ 79.05.96.70

**La Balme**
⌂ La Balme
Francinet Gut
Les Raccards
☎ 50.47.03.53
or 50.47.00.63

**Les Barmettes**
73710 Pralognan la Vanoise
⌂ des Barmettes
Mme C.Fabre

☎ 79.08.72.88
or 79.52.44.79
⌂
Mr Peccoz
☎ 79.05.25.52

**Bellachat**
74400 Les Bossons
⌂
Mr Georges Balmat
☎ 50.53.46.99

**Bellentre**
⌂
☎ 79.07.10.18

**Bellevue**
⌂ le Bellevue
Mr Leon Orset
☎ 50.78.13.24
⌂ La Hutte
☎ 50.78.09.77

**Les Bernards**
⌂ Bernards
☎ 50.93.44.39

**Bionnassay**
⌂
Mr Jean Perroud
Les Soudans
☎ 50.93.45.23
or 50.78.30.01

**Bise**
74360 Vacheresse
⌂ Le Villard
☎ 50.73.11.73

**Les Bochasses**
⌂ Mon repos
Pierre et Marie Granger

☎ 25.77.22.21

**Le Bois**
⌂ Porte de Bois Champigny
☎ 79.22.05.90

**Bonneval sur Arc**
⌂ CAF
Mr Daniel Delaplace
☎ 79.05.95.07
⌂ Le Criou
☎ 79.05.95.44
or 79.05.05.86

**Bostan**
⌂ Tornay
☎ 50.90.10.94
or 50.34.41.62

**Bramanette**
73500 Modane
⌂ de Bramanette
Mr Gerard Peccoz
☎ 79.05.25.52

**Bramans**
⌂ Les Glaciers
Mme Dupre
☎ 79.05.22.32

**Le Carro**
⌂ du Carro
Mr Gazet
☎ 84.42.72.18
☎ 79.05.95.79

**Les Cerniers sur les Giettes**
⌂
☎ 25.71.78.71

**Châlet Neuf**
⌂

☎ 25.77.12.82
or 25.71.50.93

**Chamonix**
⌂ Les pélerins
☎ 50.53.14.52
⌂ Le Chamoniard
☎ 50.53.14.09

**Champex**
⌂ Swiss Alpin Club
☎ (26).411.61
⌂ Le Belvédere
☎ (26).411.14
⌂ En plein air
☎ (26).423.50.
⌂ d'Arpette
☎ (26).412.21
or (26).428.26

**Champex d'en Haut**
⌂
☎ (26).414.23

**Les Chapieux**
⌂ de la Nova
Mr Pierre Arpin
☎ 79.07.00.36
or 79.38.91.09
⌂ L'Etape des Chapieux
Mr Joseph Pugnin
☎ 79.55.73.71
or 79.31.33.49

**Chaux Palin**
⌂
**Mr Hubert Perrin**
☎ 25.79.14.01
or 25.77.23.20

**Les Chavants**
⌂ les amis de la nature
☎ 50.54.42.65
⌂ Le Crest
Mr Jean Ladurelle
☎ 50.55.52.27

**Chésery**
⌂
☎ 25.79.14.24
⌂ Le relais
☎ 25.79.21.29
or 21.32.19.32

**La Chèvrerie**
73710 Pralognan la Vanoise
⌂ la Chevrerie
☎ 79.08.72.59

**Col de Chécroui**
11013 Courmayeur
⌂ maison Vieille
☎ (165).84.10.25

**Col de la Croix du Bonhomme**
⌂
☎ 79.38.90.32
or 79.32.10.49

**Col de la Forclaz**
⌂ du Col
☎ (26).226.88

**Col de la Vanoise**
⌂ du Col de la Vanoise
Mr Pierre Girrod
☎ 79.08.25.23
or 79.08.70.60

**Col du Palet**
⌂ du Col du Palet
Mr Recourse
☎ 79.06.34.94

**Contamines Montjoie**
74190 Le Fayet Pontet
⌂ Communal
☎ 50.47.04.04
⌂ du Nant Borrant
☎ 50.47.03.57
⌂ Les Bernards
☎ 50.93.44.39

**Courmayeur**
⌂ Elisabetta
Mr Edouardo Pennard
☎ 65.84.37.43
⌂ Svizzero
☎ (165).84.20.35

**Le Criou**
⌂ du Criou
Mr F. Mercatelli
☎ 79.05.95.44

**Les Crosets**
⌂ Portes du soleil
Mme Renee Jillabert
☎ 25.79.11.84

**La Dent d'Oche**
⌂
Mr Michel Dutruel
☎ 50.73.62.45
or 50.73.60.53

**La Dent Parrachée**
⌂ de la Dent Parrachée
☎ 79.20.32.87
⌂
☎ 79.33.05.52

**Entre Deux Eaux**
73500 Termignon
⌂ d'Entre Deux Eaux
Mr Burdin
☎ 79.05.07.43

**Entre le Lac**
⌂
Mr Porraz
☎ 79.07.94.03
or 79.08.00.29

**Les Evettes**
⌂ des Evettes
Mr Portal
☎ 79.05.96.64
or 84.42.72.18

**Evian les Bains**
74501 Evian
⌂ CIS
☎ 50.75.35.87

**La Femma**
⌂ de la Femma
☎ 79.20.33.00
or 79.20.50.85

**Ferret**
⌂ du Val Ferret
☎ (26).411.80
⌂ du Col de Fenetre
☎ (26).411.88
or (26).411.58

**Fion Chevenox**
⌂
Mr Bernard Gallay
☎ 50.72.21.30
or 50.73.65.08

**Fodze**
⌂ Monte Bianco
☎ (165).499.84

**Fond d'Aussois**
⌂ du Fond d'Aussois
☎ 79-20-32-87

**Fond des Fours**
⌂ du Fond des Fours
☎ 79.06.16.90

**La Fouly**
⌂ des glaciers
☎ (26).411.71
⌂ Edelweiss
☎ (26).426.21
⌂ Le Dolent
☎ (26).413.98

**Fort Marie Christine**
⌂ Fort Marie Christine
☎ 79.20.36.44

**Les Glaciers**
⌂ Les Glaciers
☎ 79.05.22.32

# ACCOMMODATION GUIDE

**Grand Bec**
⌂ du Grand Bec
Mr Agena
☎ 79.08.71.68

**Grassonet**
⌂ Le Nouveau Grassonet
Mlle Béatrice Clement
☎ 50.34.01.87
⌂ de l'Essarton
☎ 50.54.03.08
⌂ Le Belvédère
☎ 50.54.02.59

**Graydon**
74200 Thonon les Bains
🏛 CAF
2 rue des Italiens
☎ 50.71.81.84

**Les Houches**
Les granges
⌂ CIALC
☎ 50.54.41.81
Taconnaz
⌂ du Glacier
Mme Bernadette Chapelle
☎ 50.54.43.11

**Isertan**
⌂ d'Isertan
☎ 79.08.73.11

**Les Jeurs**
⌂ -
☎ 25.71.34.74
or 25.71.10.26

**Les Lacs Merlet**
⌂ des lacs Merlet
☎ 79.08.71.49

**Lavachey**
⌂ Mont Dolent & Locanda lavachey
☎ (165).899.62

**Le Lay**
⌂ du Télé
☎ 50.47.02.74

**La Lai**
73200 Albertville
⌂ Club Alpin Francais
4 route de la Palud
☎ 79.32.10.49

**La Leisse**
⌂ de la Leisse
Mr Maly
☎ 79.20.50.27
or 79.20.50.85

**La Martin**
⌂ de la Martin
☎ 76.06.44.32

**Merlet**
74310 Les Houches
⌂ de l'Aiguillette
Mme Denise Mollier
☎ 50.54.40.29

**Mex**
⌂ "Aux rendez-vous"
☎ (26).845.52

**Miage**
74170 Saint Gervais
⌂ de Miage
Louis Orset
☎ 50.78.07.16
or 50.93.43.06

**Les Mines d'or**
74110 Morzine
🏛 Les Chamois
Mr Francois Bard
☎ 50.79.03.60

**Les Montagnettes**
⌂ des montagnettes
☎ 79.69.32.14

**Le Mont Pourri**
⌂ du Mont Pourri
Mr Poccard
☎ 79.07.90.43

**Montroc Le Planet**
Fresserauds
⌂ Le Moulin
Mr Roger Charlet
☎ 50.54.05.37

**Montriond**
74200 Thonon les Bains
⌂ du Zauley
☎ 50.71.32.94

**La Motte**
⌂ de la Motte
Mr Henri Emprin
☎ 79.07.25.12

**Morzay**
⌂ Mermoud
☎ 50.54.60.03

**Morzine**
74110 Morzine
⌂ Le Beau Site
☎ 50.79.14.86

**Nant Borrant**
74190 Les Contamines

⌂
Mme Lucienne Mattel
☎ 50.47.03.57
or 50.47.01.20

**Nivorin**
⌂ Le Nivorin
Mme Emile Molland
☎ 50.47.03.50
⌂ Bellevue
Mr Toni Negri
☎ 50.47.00.88

**Novel**
⌂
☎ 50.76.71.31
or 50.76.73.68

**L'Orgère**
⌂ Porte de l'Orgere
☎ 79.05.11.65
or 79.62.30.54

**La Palud**
⌂ di Funivia
☎ (165).899.24

**Péclet Polset**
⌂ Peclet Polset
Mme Faure
☎ 79.08.72.13
or 79.08.72.88

**Peuty**
⌂
Mr Charles Cappi
☎ (26).223.97

**Le Petit Mont Blanc**
⌂ Le petit Mont Blanc
☎ 79.08.72.73

**Le Petit Mont Cenis**
⌂ du Petit Mont Cenis
Mme Charon
☎ 79.05.03.10

**Plaine Drause**
74390 Chatel
⌂ La Chaux des Rosées
☎ 50.73.31.19
or 50.73.25.57

**Plaisance**
⌂ de Plaisance
☎ 79.08.71.49

**Planc du Lac**
⌂ Porte de Plan du Lac
☎ 79.20.50.85
⌂
☎ 79.62.30.54

**Plan Sec**
⌂ de Plan Sec
Mme Bermond
☎ 79.20.31.31
or 79.20.32.88

**Plan Tueda**
73550 Méribel Les Allues
⌂ du Plan de Tueda
Mr Raffort
☎ 79.08.52.79

**Le Prarion**
🏠 du Prarion
☎ 50.93.47.01
or 50.93.47.04

**Prariond**
⌂ du Prariond
Mr  dupont
☎ 79.06.06.02
or 79.06.03.29

**Praz de Fort**
🏠 de Sabeinaz
☎ (26).411.68

**Rosuel**
⌂ Porte de Rosuel
☎ 79.07.94.03
or 79.62.30.54

**Le Ruitor**
⌂ du Ruitor
Mr Mercier
☎ 79.06.90.12
or 79.06.92.12

**Salanfe**
🏠 Le Choucas
Mr Jacky Pochon
☎ (26).614.38
or 25.79.14.30

**Samoëns**
74340 Samoëns
⌂ Les Couadzous
Mr Paul Granger
☎ 50.34.41.62
⌂ Les Moulins
Mr Pierre Gaborian
☎ 50.34.95.69

**Le Saut**
⌂ du Saut
Mr Lucien Raffort
☎ 79.08.71.49
or 79.08.52.44

**Séloge**
73700 Bourg Saint Maurice
⌂
Mr Paul Marchand
☎ 79.07.10.56

**Le Suffet**
⌂ du Suffet
Mr Damevin
☎ 79.05.30.17
or 79.05.35.56

**Susanfe**
🏠
☎ 25.79.16.46
Daniel Margat
☎ 24.79.29.59
or 24.21.02.33

**Termignon**
⌂ de Termignon
Mme Bantin
☎ 79.20.50.04

**Le Thabor**
⌂ du Thabor
Mr Martinez
☎ 79.20.32.13
or 79.05.24.75

**Thonon les Bains**
⌂ La Grangette
☎ 50.71.00.91

**Tignes le Lac**
🏠 du CAf
☎ 79.06.31.56
⌂ de Haute Montagne
☎ 79.06.30.02

**Tre le Champs**
⌂ La Boerne
☎ 50.54.05.77

**Trient**
⌂ du Mont Blanc

Eliane & Serge Cappi
☎ (26).246.23
🏠 du glacier
☎ (26).226.94

**Truc**
74190 Les Contamines
⌂ du Truc
Mr louis Mollard
☎ 50.93.12.43
or 50.47.02.45
⌂ Le Cugenon
Mme Bernadette Bessat
☎ 50.93.12.48
or 50.47.05.31

**Ubine**
74200 Thonon les Bains
🏠 " C Machie"
Cafe Aubert
11 Boulevard Desaix
☎ 50.71.32.94

**La Valette**
⌂ de la Valette
☎ 79.08.71.49

**Valézan**
⌂ Chez Mr Glatigny
☎ 79.55.74.85

**Vallonbrun**
⌂ de Vallonbrun
☎ 79.05.93.93
⌂
☎ 79.62.30.54

**Vallorcine**
⌂ la Scierie
Mr Patrick Ancey
☎ 50.54.61.77

**Vigny**
74110 Morzine
🏠 Le Rancho
⌂ Le Beau Site
🏠 le Guillaume
☎ 50.79.14.86

**Villaron**
⌂
☎ 79.05.95.84

# INDEX

Details of bus/train connections have been provided wherever it was possible. We suggest you refer also to the map inside the front cover.